HAMPTON-BROWN

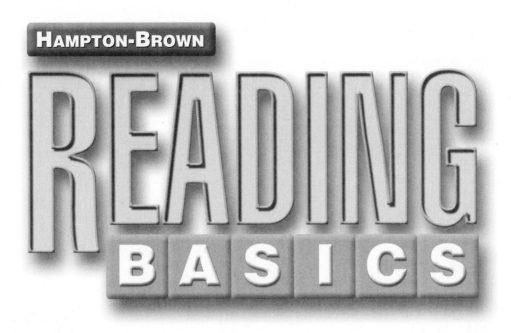

READING BASICS

Reading Practice Book

HAMPTON-BROWN

Hampton-Brown
P.O. Box 223220
Carmel, California 93922
1–800–333–3510

Printed in the United States of America
ISBN 0-7362-1236-1

03 04 05 06 07 08 09 10 9 8 7 6 5 4 3 2

Contents: Reading Practice Book

Lesson(s)

Word Work

Read each word. Then write it.

1. am _____   5. the _____

2. I _____   6. this _____

3. is _____   7. you _____

4. school _____

How to Play

1. **Make a spinner.**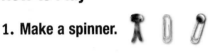

2. **Write the name of each player on a blank.**

3. **Spin.**   **Read the sentence.**

The first player to read all six sentences wins.

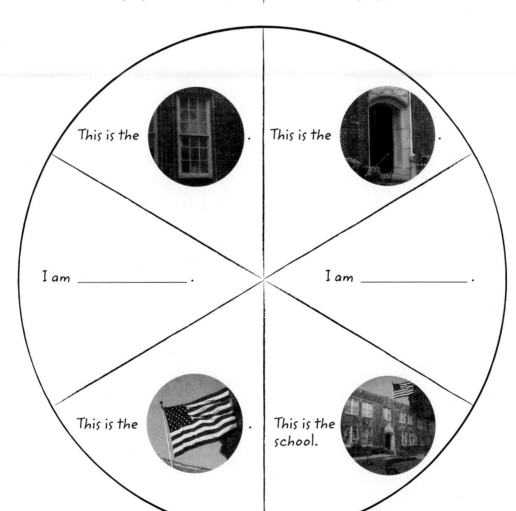

This is the _____ .   This is the _____ .

I am _____ .   I am _____ .

This is the _____ .   This is the school.

1

Word Work

Read each word. Then write it.

1. a _____   4. my _____

2. an _____   5. no _____

3. here _____   6. yes _____

1. Find the words. Circle them.

Look across. ➡

q	ⓐ	o	p	t	m
v	l	e	s	**a**	n
s	b	m	l	n	l
h	e	r	e	o	r
z	p	l	g	**m**	y
n	o	r	z	q	w
w	f	**y**	e	s	z
x	g	q	t	d	s

Write the missing words.

2. Here is ____my____ .
   my   no

3. Here is _____ .
   yes   a

4. _____ is a ▭▭▭▭▭ .
   A   Here

5. Find the words. Circle them.

Look down. ⬇

a	q	**h**	j	z	t
n	v	e	u	**n**	s
k	s	r	r	o	g
l	b	e	h	o	**y**
r	**a**	i	z	e	e
x	f	s	**m**	r	s
w	g	o	y	e	q
p	u	z	e	l	v

Write the missing words.

6. This is ____an____ .
   an   yes

7. _____ is a .
   Here   My

8. This is _____ .
   no   a

Letters and Sounds

Study the new letters and sounds.

Ss   **Mm**   **Ff**   **Hh**   **Tt**   **Aa**

Say the name of each picture below. What letter spells the <u>first</u> sound you hear? Circle the letter.

1.

t   (h)   a

4.

f   h   a

7.

a   m   t

2.

a   h   s

5.

a   m   s

8.

a   s   m

3.

h   f   s

6.

t   h   a

9.

t   h   a

Letters and Sounds

Say the name of each picture below. What letter spells the
<u>first</u> sound you hear? Write the letter.

1.

____s____

2.

____

3.

____

4.

____

5.

____

6.

____

7.

____

8.

____

9.

____

10.

____

11.

____

12.

____

13.

____

14.

____

15.

____

Name _____

Word Work

Read each word. Then write it.

1. at _____
2. it _____
3. look _____
4. of _____

5. on _____
6. see _____
7. show _____
8. where _____

Write the missing letters.

9. **Which words have a t?**

   <u>a</u> <u>t</u>　　___ ___

10. **Which words have 2 letters?**

    ___ ___　　___ ___

    ___ ___　　___ ___

11. **Which word has 3 letters?**

    ___ ___ ___

12. **Which words have 4 letters?**

    ___ ___ ___ ___

    ___ ___ ___ ___

13. **Which word has 5 letters?**

    ___ ___ ___ ___ ___

14. **Which words start with o?**

    ___ ___　　___ ___

15. **Which word has an f?**

    ___ ___

Write the missing words.

16. I _____*see*_____ you.
    　　see　*where*

17. Carlos, _____ at this!
    　　　　show　*look*

18. Is this the school?

    Yes, _____ is.
    　　　it　*at*

19. _____ me the school.
    　Show　*Where*

20. _____ is the ?
    　Look　*Where*

21. I am _____ school.
    　　　　at　*of*

22. This is a _____
    　　　　　　　　of　*show*
    the school.

23. The is _____ the .
    　　　it　*on*

Words with Short *a*

Read each word. Draw a line to match the word and the picture.

1.

hat

ham

2.

fat

mat

Write the missing words.

3.

This is a _____ *hat* _____.
     ham   *hat*

4.

Maylin is _____ school.
           at   *sat*

5.

Here is the _____.
            fat   *mat*

6.

I _____ Carlos.
   Sam   *am*

7.

This is a _____.
           ham   *hat*

8.

You _____ at the .
     at   *sat*

Words with Short *a*

Write the missing *a*. Then read the words in each list.
How are the words different?

1. _a_ m

    S___m

    h___m

2. ___t

    h___t

    s___t

3. ___t

    f___t

    m___t

What word completes each sentence and tells about the picture? Spell the word.

4. Here is my _h_ _a_ _t_ .

5. I am ___ ___ ___ .

6. This is a ___ ___ ___ .

7. I am ___ ___ school.

8. I ___ ___ Carlos.

9. I ___ ___ ___ on the .

10. Sam ___ ___ ___ a .

11. Look at the ___ ___ ___ .

12. I ___ ___ at the .

13. You ___ ___ ___ at the .

Word Work

Read each word. Then write it.

1. are _____
2. good _____
3. he _____
4. she _____

5. some _____
6. time _____
7. who _____
8. your _____

Write the missing letters.

9. **Which words have 4 letters?**

g o o d ___ ___ ___ ___

___ ___ ___ ___   ___ ___ ___ ___

10. **Which word has an a?**

___ ___ ___

11. **Which word has 2 letters?**

___ ___

12. **Which words have 3 letters?**

___ ___ ___

___ ___ ___

___ ___ ___

13. **Which word has a g?**

___ ___ ___ ___

14. **Which word has a t?**

___ ___ ___ ___

Write the missing word.

15. Here ____are____ two 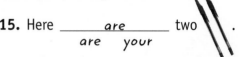 .

    are   your

16.  What _____ is it?

    some   time

17.  Where is _____ ?

    are   she

18. _____ is he?

    Good   Who

19. Is this _____ 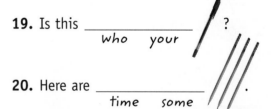 ?

    who   your

20. Here are _____ .

    time   some

21. _____ is Carlos.

    Some   He

22. This is a _____  .

    good   are

23. Here is _____ hat.

    who   your

Letters and Sounds

Study the new letters and sounds.

Nn   **Ll**   **Pp**   **Gg**   **Ii**

Say the name of each picture below. What letter spells the
<u>first</u> sound you hear? Circle the letter.

1.

   (n)   f   s

2.

   l   p   n

3.

   s   l   n

4.

   t   h   i

5.

   f   m   p

6.

   g   p   l

7.

   l   g   f

8.

   p   f   i

9.

   l   n   t

10.

    l   p   n

11.

    l   g   n

12.

    t   g   a

Letters and Sounds

Say the name of each picture below.
Write the missing letters.

1.

_h_ _a_ _m_

2.

___ ___ ___

3.

___ _i_ ___

4.

_s_ _i_ ___

5.

___ _i_ ___

6.

_m_ ___ ___

7.

___ ___ ___

8.

___ ___ _m_ _p_

9.

___ ___ ___

10.

_m_ ___ ___

11.

___ _i_ ___

12.

___ ___ ___

Word Work

Read each word. Then write it.

1. answer _____   5. with _____

2. point _____   6. work _____

3. read _____   7. write _____

4. to _____

Write the missing words.

8. **Which word has 6 letters?**

   <u>a</u> <u>n</u> <u>s</u> <u>w</u> <u>e</u> <u>r</u>

9. **Which words have an <u>n</u>?**

   __ __ __ __ __ __

   __ __ __ __ __

10. **Which words have 5 letters?**

    __ __ __ __ __

    __ __ __ __ __

11. **Which words have 4 letters?**

    __ __ __ __

    __ __ __ __

    __ __ __ __

12. **Which word has a <u>p</u>?**

    __ __ __ __ __

13. **Which word has 2 letters?**

    __ __

Write the missing words.

14. Point _____<u>to</u>_____ the .

with   to

15. I _____ the .

to   read

16. I show my _____.

work   with

17. I write the _____.

answer   read

18. _____ to the answer.

With   Point

19. I work _____ you.

to   with

20. _____ on the _____.

Write   To

21. Is this your _____ ?

with   answer

22. _____ with a /.

Write   To

11

Words with Short *a* and *i*

Read each word. Draw a line to match the word and the picture.

1.

pan

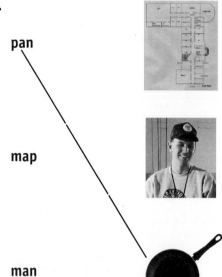

map

man

2.

pin

sit

pig

Write the missing words.

3.

She has a

__hat__.
hat   mat

4.

This is a

_____.
pan   ham

5.

This is a

_____.
fan   man

6.

_____ it!
Pin   Hit

7.

This is a

_____.
pin   pig

8.

He is a

_____.
man   mat

9.

This is a

_____.
pan   pig

10.

You _____
sit   hit

in a .

Words with Short *a* and *i*

Write the missing letters. Then read the words in each list.
How are the words different?

1.   _h_ ___ ___

  ___ ___ ___

  ___ ___ ___

2.   _p_ ___ ___

  ___ ___ ___

  ___ ___ ___

Read each question. What word goes in the answer? Spell the word.
Then circle the correct picture.

3. Where is the pig?

The _p_ _i_ _g_ is here.

4. Where is the pan?

Here is the ___ ___ ___.

5. Where is Sam? ___ ___ ___ is here.

6. Who hit it?

Carlos ___ ___ ___ it.

7. Who has the hat?

She ___ ___ ___ the hat.

8. Who is the man? He is a ___ ___ ___.

Word Work

Read each word. Then write it.

1. call _____
2. name _____
3. need _____
4. number _____
5. to _____
6. what _____

Write the missing letters.

7. **Which word has 2 letters?**

   _t_ _o_

8. **Which words have 4 letters?**

   __ __ __ __

   __ __ __ __

   __ __ __ __

   __ __ __ __

9. **Which word has 6 letters.**

   __ __ __ __ __ __

10. **Which words have a _t_?**

    __ __

    __ __ __ __

11. **Which words have an _n_?**

    __ __ __ __

    __ __ __ __

    __ __ __ __ __ __

12. **Which word has an _l_ at the end?**

    __ __ __ __

Write the missing word.

13. My _____name_____ is Ana.

    number   name

14. I _____ to show my work.

    what   need

15. My phone _____ is 678-5335.

    number   name

16. I can _____ Carlos.

    call   what

17. _____ is your name?

    What   Need

18. I need _____ see you.

    name   to

Circle each number.

19. m   f   85   p   g

     19   i   20   a   n

      s   50   h   t   7

Letters and Sounds

Study the new letters and sounds.

Rr **Dd** **Cc** **Vv** **Oo**

Say the name of each picture below. **What letter spells the first sound you hear?** Circle the letter.

1.

m (d) o

2.

r v n

3.

l h c

4.

a r d

5.

c n v

6.

o r i

7.

l g c

8.

h t p

9.

r d f

10.

a v l

11.

d a s

12.

v i h

13.

c p t

14.

o m v

15.

o d i

16.

d g v

Letters and Sounds

Say the name of each picture below.
Write the missing letters.

1.

   <u>d</u>   <u>o</u>   <u>t</u>

2.

   ___   ___   ___

3.

   ___   <u>o</u>   ___

4.

   ___   ___   ___

5.

   ___   ___   ___

6.

   <u>f</u>   <u>l</u>   ___   ___

7.

   <u>c</u>   <u>l</u>   ___   <u>s</u>   <u>s</u>

8.

   ___   <u>a</u>   ___

9.

   ___   <u>a</u>   ___

10.

    ___   ___   <u>m</u>   <u>p</u>

11.

    ___   ___   ___

12.

    ___   ___   ___

Word Work

Read each word. Then write it.

1. do _____
2. does _____
3. for _____
4. help _____
5. in _____

6. like _____
7. me _____
8. picture _____
9. will _____

How to Play

1. Play with a partner. **Each partner chooses a sign.** X O

2. Partner 1 reads a word and marks the square with a sign.

3. Then Partner 2 takes a turn.

4. Get 3 Xs or Os in a row to win.

A.

do	help	like
in	does	will
me	picture	for

B.

picture	like	in
does	me	for
will	do	help

C.

help	does	me
do	will	for
like	in	picture

D.

does	will	help
picture	me	in
for	like	do

Name _____

Words with Short *a*, *i*, and *o*

Read each word. Draw a line to the correct picture.

1.

mop

map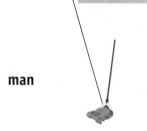

man

2.

pan

pig

pin

3.

pot

dot

mop

Write the missing words.

4.

This is a

___van___.

van   man

5.

I like this

_____.

map   man

6.

The _____

pot   dot

is hot.

7.

Here is a good

_____.

map   mop

8.

●

This is a

_____.

not   dot

9.

This lamp is

_____ the .

am   on

© Hampton-Brown

18

Words with Short *a*, *i*, and *o*

Write the missing letters. Then read the words in each list.
How are the words different?

1.   c _ _

   _ _ _

   _ _ _

2.   p _ _

   _ _ _

   _ _ _

3.   h _ _

   _ _ _

   _ _ _

Read each question and the answer. Write the missing words. Then circle the correct picture.

4. Is this pot hot?

No, the _p_ _o_ _t_ is _n_ _o_ _t_ hot.

5. Is this your cap?

Yes, it is my ___ ___ ___.

6. Where is the mop?

The ___ ___ ___ is here.

7. Where can I sit?

You can ___ ___ ___ here.

8. Point to the dot.

The ___ ___ ___ is here!

9. Do you like the hat?

Yes, I like the ___ ___ ___.

Name _____

Word Work

Read each word. Then write it.

1. around _____   4. too _____

2. can _____   5. we _____

3. play _____

Write the missing letters.

6. **Which words have 3 letters?**

   _c_ _a_ _n_

   ___ ___ ___

7. **Which word has 6 letters?**

   ___ ___ ___ ___ ___ ___

8. **Which word has 4 letters?**

   ___ ___ ___ ___

9. **Which word has an r?**

   ___ ___ ___ ___ ___ ___

10. **Which word that has 2 letters?**

    ___ ___

11. **Which word has a t?**

    ___ ___ ___

12. **Which word has a d?**

    ___ ___ ___ ___ ___

13. **Which words have an n?**

    ___ ___ ___ ___ ___ ___

Write the missing word.

14. Can you ___play___ ?
    play   we

15. Yes, I _____ play.
    around   can

16. Dan and I play, _____!
    too   can

17. _____ play at school.
    Too   We

18. Can you _____ the ___?
    around   we

19. Yes, we _____!
    can   around

20. I can, _____.
    we   too

21. Can you _____ ○?
    around   play

22. Yes, _____ can.
    too   we

Letters and Sounds

Study the new letters and sounds.

Jj   **Bb**   **Ww**   **Kk**   **Ee**

How to Play Bingo

1. Write the letters from the box.

2. Then listen to the word your teacher reads.

3. Put a ⬭ on the letter that stands for the first sound in the word.

4. The first player to cover all the letters in a row is the winner.

Letters to Write

a	i	p
b	j	r
b	j	s
c	k	t
d	k	v
e	l	w
f	m	w
g	n	
h	o	

Words to Read

am	got	lot	top
bat	hit	mat	van
big	it	not	win
can	jam	on	wig
dot	jog	pin	
egg	kid	red	
fat	kit	sit	

Letters and Sounds

Say the name of each picture below.
Write the missing letters.

1.

   p o t

2.

   __ __ __

3.

   __ __ __

4.

   __ g g

5.

   __ e s t

6.

   __ __ __

7.

   __ __ __

8.

   __ o g

9.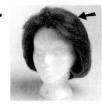

   __ i g

10.

    __ i t

11.

    __ e __

12.

    __ e __

Word Work

Read each word. Then write it.

1. feel _____   4. how _____

2. has _____   5. put _____

3. have _____   6. they _____

Write the missing letters.

7. Which words start with <u>h</u>?

   h a s   ___ ___ ___

   ___ ___ ___ ___

8. Which word has a <u>p</u>?

   ___ ___ ___

9. Which words have 3 letters?

   ___ ___ ___   ___ ___ ___

   ___ ___ ___

10. Which words have 4 letters?

    ___ ___ ___ ___   ___ ___ ___ ___

    ___ ___ ___ ___

11. Which word has an <u>f</u>?

    ___ ___ ___ ___

12. Which word has a <u>v</u>?

    ___ ___ ___ ___

13. Which word has an <u>l</u>?

    ___ ___ ___ ___

14. Which word has an <u>s</u>?

    ___ ___ ___

Write the missing word.

15. ___How___ do you feel?
    Put   How

16.  I _____ good.
    feel   put

17. I _____ bad.
    feel   has

18. 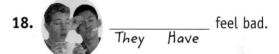 _____ feel bad.
    They   Have

19. Do you _____ a ?
    have   they

20. She _____ a kit.
    how   has

21. _____ the kit here.
    How   Put

Words with Short *a*, *i*, *o*, and *e*

Read each word. Draw a line to the correct picture.

1.
jam

ham

hat

2.
pen

ten

men

3.
cat

bat

bed

Write the missing words.

4.

Here are two

_____men_____.

men   ten

7.

This is a good

_____.

pan   pen

10.

Here is a

_____.

bed   Ed

5.

• • • • •
• • • •

There are

_____ dots.

ten   pen

8.

He can _____

hot   hit

the ⚬.

11.

I do _____

dot   not

like to play.

6.
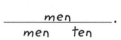
My pet is a

_____.

pig   pin

9.

This is my

_____.

cap   map

12.

Put it in the

_____.

pot   pat

Words with Short *a*, *i*, *o*, and *e*

**Write the missing letters. Then read the words in each list.
How are the words different?**

1.   m ___ ___

 ___ ___ ___

  ___ ___ ___

2.   c ___ ___

  ___ ___ ___

  ___ ___ ___

3.   p ___ ___

  ___ ___ ___

 ___ ___ ___

Write the missing words.

4.

This is my p e n .

5.

Look at the ___ ___ ___.

6.

Here is my ___ ___ ___.

7.

Carlos has a ___ ___ ___.

8.

Do you like my

___ ___ s t ?

9.

This is a f l ___ ___.

10.

I like to ___ ___ ___.

11.

I ___ ___ ___

at my ___ ___ ___ ___.

12.

Where is my ___ ___ ___?

Word Work

Read each word. Then write it.

1. and _____
2. don't _____
3. food _____

4. not _____
5. that _____

Write the missing letters.

6. Which words have 3 letters?

    _a_ _n_ _d_

    ___ ___ ___

7. Which words have an **a**?

    ___ ___ ___

    ___ ___ ___ ___

8. Which word has an **f**?

    ___ ___ ___ ___

9. Which words have an **n**?

    ___ ___ ___

    ___ ___ ___ , ___

    ___ ___ ___

10. Which words end in a **t**?

    ___ ___ ___ , ___

    ___ ___ ___

    ___ ___ ___

Write the missing word.

11. I like ___*that*___ food.
    and   that

12. I do _____ like that food.
    and   not

13. I like the  _____ .
    and   food

14. I _____ like ⬤ .
    that   don't

15. This _____ is good for you.
    and   food

16. Is this food?

    No, it is _____ food.
    and   not

17. This is ⬤ _____ a ⬤ .
    and   don't

18. What is _____ ?
    not   that

19. This _____ is good.
    and   food

Name _____

How to Write a Statement

A **statement** tells something.

It starts with a <u>capital letter</u>.

It ends with a <u>period</u>.

Examples: This is Lakeside School.

There are many students here.

Read each statement. Is it written correctly? If so, put a ✔ next to it. If not, correct it.

1. ✔ We are at school.

2. ☐ It is time for lunch.

3. ☐ She is in the cafeteria

4. ☐ He has some pizza.

5. ☐ you can have some food.

6. ☐ this is a salad

7. ☐ This is a sandwich.

8. ☐ Now it is time for class.

Write each statement correctly.

9. Ron is here

<u>Ron is here.</u>

10. Kim is here, too

_____

11. here is the food

_____

12. I like the taco and beans

_____

13. my friends don't like bagels

_____

14. I have a cookie

_____

15. we have some milk

_____

16. the food is good

_____

Word Work

Read each word. Then write it.

1. give _____   **3.** think _____

2. take _____

How to Play

1. Get 25 paper clips. **Play with a partner.**

1 **2**

2. Use an eraser or other small object as your game piece.
Use a coin to show how many spaces to move.

 Heads = 1 space   Tails = 2 spaces

3. Read the sentence. Then do what it says.
The player with more paper clips at the end wins.

FINISH

Give 1
paper clip.

Take 5
paper clips.

START

Give 3
paper clips.

Take 1
paper clip.

Take 1
paper clip.

Give 5
paper clips.

Give 3
paper clips.

Take 2
paper clips.

Give 2
paper clips.

Take 4
paper clips.

Take 6
paper clips.

Give 7
paper clips.

Letters and Sounds

Study the new letters and sounds.

Zz   Yy   Uu   Qq   Xx

How to Play Bingo

1. Write the letters from the box.

2. Then listen to the word your teacher reads.

3. Put a ◯ on the letter that stands for the first sound in the word.

4. The first player to cover all the letters in a row is the winner.

Letters to Write

a	j	s
b	k	t
c	l	u
d	m	v
e	n	w
f	o	y
g	p	z
h	q	
i	r	

Words to Read

am	him	on	van
bat	in	pen	wig
cot	jam	quit	yes
dot	kid	red	zip
egg	lot	sat	
fan	map	ten	
got	not	up	

Letters and Sounds

Say the name of each picture below.
Write the missing letters.

1.

   $\underline{l}$ $\underline{\;e\;}$ $\underline{\;g\;}$

2.

   $\underline{\quad}$ $\underline{\quad}$ $\underline{\;i\;}$ $\underline{\;l\;}$ $\underline{\;t\;}$

3.

   $\underline{\quad}$ $\underline{\quad}$

4.

   $\underline{\quad}$ $\underline{\quad}$ $\underline{\quad}$

5.

   $\underline{\quad}$ $\underline{\;u\;}$ $\underline{\quad}$

6.

   $\underline{\quad}$ $\underline{\quad}$ $\underline{\quad}$

7.

   $\underline{\quad}$ $\underline{\;u\;}$ $\underline{\quad}$

8.

   $\underline{\quad}$ $\underline{\;u\;}$ $\underline{\quad}$

9.

   $\underline{\quad}$ $\underline{\quad}$ $\underline{\quad}$

10.

    $\underline{\quad}$ $\underline{\quad}$ $\underline{\quad}$

11.

    $\underline{\quad}$ $\underline{\;u\;}$ $\underline{\quad}$

12.

    $\underline{\quad}$ $\underline{\quad}$

Word Work

Read each word. Then write it.

1. both _____
2. get _____
3. little _____
4. old _____
5. them _____

6. these _____
7. things _____
8. those _____
9. very _____
10. which _____

Read the sentence. Write the missing word on the blank and in the crossword puzzle.

DOWN ↓

1. I like ___*both*___ the shorts
   and the T-shirt.

3. Which _____ do you like?

5. I like _____ blue shorts that I have.

6. My pants are _____.
   I need new ones.

8. I like the pants and the shorts.
   I like both of _____.

ACROSS ➡

2. Carlos will _____ a T-shirt.

4. Carlos, _____ caps do you like?

5. I like _____ green
   caps on the table.

7. I like the _____
   T-shirt on the lion!

9. My T-shirt is not _____ old.

31

Words with Short *a*, *i*, *o*, *e*, and *u*

Read each word. Draw a line to the correct picture.

1.

cot

cat

cap

2.

up

cup

cut

3.

ax

ox

box

Write the missing words.

4.

I can _z_ _i_ _p_ it.

6.

I like this old

___ ___ ___ ___ .

8.

I have ___ ___ ___ pins.

5.

This is my ___ ___ ___.

7.

Do you like my little

___ ___ ___?

9.

Is this a pig?

___ ___ ___!

Words with Short *a, i, o, e,* and *u*

Write the missing letters. Then read the words in each list.
How are the words different?

1.

_u_ _ _

_ _ _

_ _ _

2.

_c_ _ _

_ _ _

_ _ _

3.

_p_ _ _

_ _ _

_ _ _

Write the missing words.

4.

There is _m_ _i_ _l_ _k_

in my _c_ _u_ _p_ .

5.

Is this my _ _ _ ?

6.

He _ _ _ it.

7.

I have a

_ _ _ _ .

8.

She can _ _ _ it.

9.

Here is an _ _ _ .

10.

There is a bug on my

_ _ _ .

11.

He has an _ _ .

12.

The lamp is not in the

_ _ _ .

Name _____

Word Work

Read each word. Then write it.

1. great _____   **3.** soon   _____

2. later _____   **4.** tomorrow _____

Write the missing word in each sentence.

5. I need your work _____tomorrow_____ .
       great   tomorrow

6. That is too _____ ! I think I need help!
       soon   later

7. I can help you _____ at 4:00.
       great   later

8. _____ !
       Great   Soon

9. See you _____ .
       later   great

10. See you _____ !
        great   soon

Work with 2 partners.

Act out the story.

Read the sentences with your group.

How to Write a Question

A **question** asks something.

It starts with a <u>capital letter</u>.

It ends with a <u>question mark</u>.

Examples: <u>Is</u> this your school<u>?</u>

<u>Are</u> Carlos and Maylin here<u>?</u>

Read each question. Is it written correctly? If so, put a ✔ next to it. If not, correct it.

1. ✔ Is the basketball game on Tuesday?

2. ☐ what is your number

3. ☐ Are they here

4. ☐ Can he play on Wednesday?

5. ☐ do you like basketball?

6. ☐ Will you call me later?

7. ☐ Does Carlos want to play on Sunday

8. ☐ Who is with Maylin?

Write each question correctly.

9. is this the basketball court

   Is this the basketball court?

10. where are my friends

   _____

11. is it 4:00

   _____

12. do you like basketball

   _____

13. can you play on Tuesday

   _____

14. does carlos like basketball

   _____

15. which basketball do you need

   _____

16. can we get the basketball on Friday

   _____

Word Work

Read each word. Then write it.

1. book _____
2. boy _____
3. day _____
4. girl _____

5. group _____
6. letters _____
7. night _____
8. year _____

Write the missing letters.

9. **Which words have an <u>l</u>?**

    _g_ _i_ _r_ _l_

    __ __ __ __ __ __ __

10. **Which words have 5 letters?**

    __ __ __ __ __

    __ __ __ __ __

11. **Which word has a <u>p</u>?**

    __ __ __ __ __

12. **Which words have a <u>b</u>?**

    __ __ __ __

    __ __ __

Write the name of each thing.

13.

    letters
    letters   day

14.

    girl   book

15.

    year   night

16.

    boy   girl

17.

    girl   book

18.

    night   group

How to Write an Exclamation

An **exclamation** shows a strong feeling.

It starts with a <u>capital letter</u>.

It ends with an <u>exclamation mark</u>.

Examples: <u>Help me!</u>

<u>Look at that!</u>

Read each exclamation. Is it written correctly? If so, put a ✔ next to it. If not, correct it.

1. ✔ See you soon!

2. ☐ listen

3. ☐ Here they are

4. ☐ This is good work!

5. ☐ I like that food

6. ☐ call me tomorrow

7. ☐ Carlos is here

8. ☐ great!

Write each exclamation correctly.

9. we can do that in October

<u>We can do that in October!</u>

10. this book is great

_____

11. see you later

_____

12. Carlos likes this one

_____

13. this is great work

_____

14. call me on Friday

_____

15. he looks great

_____

16. June will be fun

_____

Words to Know

READ AND WRITE

Read each word. Then write it.

1. new _____ 2. many _____ 3. one _____

4. from _____ 5. first _____ 6. then _____

7. go _____ 8. next _____ 9. there _____

10. home _____

WORD WORK

Read each sentence. Find the new words in the box.
Write the words on the lines.

11. These 2 words have 3 letters.

    ____new____   ____one____

12. These 2 words begin with **th**.

    _____   _____

13. These 3 words have an **m**.

    _____   _____

    _____

14. This word rhymes with **where**.

    _____

15. This word is the opposite of **stop**.

    _____

16. These 4 words have an **o**.

    _____   _____

    _____   _____

17. These 3 words tell "when."

    _____   _____

    _____

18. These 5 words have 4 letters each.

    _____   _____

    _____   _____

    _____

SHORT A, SHORT O

Words with Short <u>a</u> and Short <u>o</u>

Name each picture. Write the name.

1.

hat

2.

_____

3.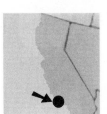

_____

4.

_____

5.

_____

6.

_____

7.

_____

8.

_____

Now read the story. Circle the words with short <u>a</u> or short <u>o</u>.
Write them in the chart. Write each word one time.

I See a (Van)

I see a van.

It has a lot of things in it!

I see a map and a box in the van.

I see a mop and a fan in the van.

I see some pots and pans, too.

Is Tom in the van?

Tom is not in the van. There is no room!

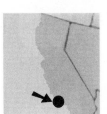	
9. ____van____	15. _____
10. _____	16. _____
11. _____	17. _____
12. _____	18. _____
13. _____	19. _____
14. _____	20. _____

SHORT A, SHORT O

More Words with Short a and Short o

Read each word. Which picture goes with the word? Write its letter.

1. cot __G__   2. cap ___   3. fan ___   4. top ___   5. jog ___

6. bag ___   7. fog ___   8. dot ___   9. van ___   10. rag ___

11. hop ___   12. bat ___   13. nap ___   14. hat ___   15. sad ___

A.
B.
C.
D.
E.

F.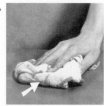
G.
H.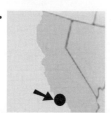
I.
J.

K.
L.
M.
N.
O.

Name each picture below. Which word or words above rhyme with the picture name? Write the words on the lines.

16. _cap_ _____

17. _____

18. _____

19. _____

20. _____

21.  _____

22. _____

23.  _____

© Hampton-Brown

40

COMPREHENSION

Build Reading Fluency

Some sentences tell something. Other sentences show strong feeling.

**This sentence tells something.
It ends with a period.**

> Lupe is new at Lakeside School.

**This sentence shows a strong feeling.
It ends with an exclamation mark.**

> Lupe is glad to have 2 new friends!

LISTEN AND LEARN TO READ

Listen to the different kinds of sentences.

New at School

Lupe is new at Lakeside School.
First she has science lab with Pat and Ron.
Pat helps Lupe.
Next they have P.E. class.
Pat and Lupe go fast. Ron does not go fast.
He has a cold and has to stop!
Then Pat, Lupe, and Ron go to lunch.
They have a lot of hot soup.
At last it is time to go home.
Lupe is glad to have 2 new friends!

PRACTICE

Now read the sentences above. Work with a partner.

Say each kind of sentence with the right expression.

See how your reading improves!

Words to Know

READ AND WRITE

Read each word. Then write it.

1. large _____	2. open _____	3. small _____
4. different _____	5. long _____	6. same _____
7. make _____	8. eat _____	9. move _____
10. something _____		

WORD WORK

Read the clue. Write the word in the chart.
Then write the word again in the sentence.

What to Look For	Word	Sentence
11. starts with **o**	<u>o</u> <u>p</u> <u>e</u> <u>n</u>	I _____open_____ my lunch.
12. starts with **sm**	_ _ _ _ _	It is in a _____ bag.
13. has **ff**	_ _ _ _ _ _ _ _ _	Your bag is _____ .
14. means "big"	_ _ _ _ _	You have a _____ bag.
15. ends with **ve**	_ _ _ _	Please _____ over.
16. has 3 letters	_ _ _	It is time to _____ .
17. has the word **some** in it	_ _ _ _ _ _ _ _ _	I want _____ hot.
18. rhymes with **song**	_ _ _ _	I like _____ noodles.
19. ends with **me**	_ _ _ _	Our food is not the _____ .
20. rhymes with **take**	_ _ _ _	You _____ great food.

Words with Short i and Short u

Name each picture. Write the name.

1.

pin

2.

_____

3.

_____

4.

_____

5.

_____

6.

_____

7.

_____

8.

_____

Now read the story. Circle the words with short i or short u.
Write them in the chart. Write each word one time.

Just Great!

Sam needs something to eat.

He rips open a bag of chips.

The chips are good, but not great.

Sam cuts a bit of ham and
slaps it on a bun.

The ham is good, but not great.

Mom comes in.

She gets a cup of ice cream.

She adds lots of nuts.

Sam grins. Yes! That's great!

9. ___Just___	15. _____
10. _____	16. _____
11. _____	17. _____
12. _____	18. _____
13. _____	19. _____
14. _____	20. _____
	21. _____

SHORT I, SHORT U

More Words with Short i and Short u

Read each word. Which picture goes with the word? Write its letter.

1. cup _G_   2. fin ___   3. pump ___   4. hit ___   5. sit ___

6. rug ___   7. disk ___   8. nut ___   9. pig ___   10. dig ___

11. sun ___   12. pin ___   13. cut ___   14. lid ___   15. bun ___

A.  B.  C.  D.  E.

F.  G.  H.  I.  J.

K.  L.  M.  N.  O.

Name each picture below. Which word or words above rhyme with the picture name? Write the words on the lines.

16.   _bun_
_____

17.   _____
_____

18.   _____
_____

19.   _____

20.   _____

21.   _____

22.   _____
_____

Build Reading Fluency

When you read, pause between groups of words that go together.

Kim likes hot dogs / for lunch.

She cooks / a batch of hot dogs / in a big pot.

LISTEN AND LEARN TO READ

Listen to the story. Which groups of words does the reader say together?
Where does he pause? When you hear a pause, write a **/** .

Example: Kim likes hot dogs **/** for lunch.

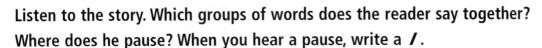

Something Good for Lunch

Kim likes hot dogs for lunch.
She cooks a batch of hot dogs in a big pot.
Next Kim chops some small onions.
She opens a large bag of buns.
She fills the buns with hot dogs, mustard, and onions.
She opens a bag of chips, too.
She pours a cup of punch.
This is too much food to eat!
Kim calls Mitch.
Then they sit and eat a great lunch!

PRACTICE

Now read the story to a partner. Read groups of words together.
Pause when you see a **/** .

HIGH FREQUENCY WORDS

Words to Know

READ AND WRITE

Read each word. Then write it.

1. carry _____	2. face _____	3. say _____
4. learn _____	5. find _____	6. use _____
7. study _____	8. love _____	9. want _____
10. when _____		

Find each word in the box. Write it on the line.

11. This word has 2 **r**'s.

_____

12. This word means "like a lot."

_____

WORD WORK

Read each sentence. Find the new words in the box.
Write the words on the lines.

13. These 3 words have 5 letters each.

___carry___   ___learn___

___study___

14. This word rhymes with **day**.

_____

15. This word has an **i**.

_____

16. This word starts with **st**.

_____

17. These 3 words end with **e**.

_____   _____

_____

18. This word ends with **nt**.

_____

19. This word rhymes with **then**.

_____

20. These 2 words start with **l**.

_____   _____

SHORT _E_ AND _CK_

Words with Short <u>e</u>

Read each word. Which picture goes with the word? Write its letter.

1. hen ⟶ F
2. check ⟶ __
3. net ⟶ __
4. pet ⟶ __
5. bed ⟶ __
6. chest ⟶ __
7. pen ⟶ __
8. vet ⟶ __
9. egg ⟶ __
10. bench ⟶ __
11. stretch ⟶ __
12. send ⟶ __

A.

B.

C.

D.

E.

F.

G.

H.

I.

J.

K.

L.

Name each picture below. Which words above rhyme with the picture name? Write the words on the lines.

13.  pet
   _____
   _____

14. _____
   _____

CK AND DOUBLE CONSONANTS

Final ll, ss, zz, ck

Read each word. Which picture goes with the word? Write its letter.

1. chick A   2. pill ___   3. bell ___   4. fizz ___

5. check ___   6. jazz ___   7. kiss ___   8. spill ___

9. rock ___   10. sick ___   11. dress ___   12. hill ___

A.    B.    C.    D.

E.    F.    G.    H.

I.    J.    K.    L.

Name each picture below. What is the last sound? Find the words above that have the same sound at the end. Write the words on the lines.

13.  _____
_____
_____

14.  _____
_____
_____

COMPREHENSION

Build Reading Fluency

Some sentences ask something. Other sentences show strong feeling.

This sentence asks a question.
It ends with a question mark.

Do you want to send something **?**

This sentence shows a strong feeling.
It ends with an exclamation mark.

Then he hops on his bike and … zip **!**

LISTEN AND LEARN TO READ

Listen to the reader's voice. Listen for sentences that ask
a question or show a strong feeling.

Let Ben Take It

Ben is a bike messenger.
Do you want to send something?
Ben can get it there fast.
Just tell him where it must go.
He gets his map.
He uses it to find a shop.
Then he hops on his bike and … zip!
He is off like a jet.
Ben can carry a lot of different things:
food, pictures, letters, flowers.
They fit in the big bag on his back.
Ben loves his job.
When you want to send something,
let Ben take it!

PRACTICE

Now read the sentences to a partner. See how your reading improves!

Words to Know

READ AND WRITE

Read each word. Then write it.

1. all _____   2. more _____   3. second _____

4. out _____   5. leave _____   6. enough _____

7. two _____   8. three _____   9. without _____

10. says _____

Find the new words in the box. Write the words on the lines.

11. These 2 words have 6 letters each.

_____   _____

12. These 2 words begin with **s**.

_____   _____

WORD WORK

Work with a partner. Follow the steps.

① Read aloud each new word in the box.

② Your partner writes the word.

③ Have your partner read the word to you.

④ Now you write the words on the lines below.

⑤ Read the words to your partner.

13. _____   18. _____

14. _____   19. _____

15. _____   20. _____

16. _____   21. _____

17. _____   22. _____

Words with Blends

Name each picture. Write the name.

1.

spots

2.

_____

3.

_____

4.

_____

5.

_____

6.

_____

7.

_____

8.

_____

Now read the story. Circle the words that go in the chart.
Write them in the chart.

Pack for (Camp)

Jim packs his bag for camp. He
needs enough stuff to last 5 days.
He packs:

• 1 tent and a mat to sleep on

• 2 swim trunks for his swim class

• a belt, 4 snacks, 10 socks, 1 brush,
and more!

He can smash it all in the bag, but he
can not lift the bag! Jim has to pack
two bags for camp.

Starts with <u>st</u>	Ends with <u>st</u>
9. _____	13. _____
Starts with <u>tr</u>	**Ends with <u>nt</u>**
10. _____	14. _____
Starts with <u>cl</u>	**Ends with <u>mp</u>**
11. _____	15. _____Camp_____
Starts with <u>sn</u>	**Ends with <u>lt</u>**
12. _____	16. _____

Words with Digraphs

Name each picture. Write the name.

1.

_____trash_____

2.

_____

3.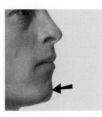

_____

4.

_____

5.

_____

6.

_____

7.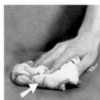

_____

8.

_____

Now read the story. Circle the words that go in the chart.
Write them in the chart. Write each word one time.

A Trip to (the) (Shop)

Dad and I go out to a shop. I think it sells great shells. We can bring some to Mom. I pick six shells and Dad pays cash. There is one more thing we want to do – find some fresh fish to eat. When we go home, Dad gives Mom the shells. Mom loves them and puts them on a shelf. What a great day!

Starts with <u>th</u>	Starts with <u>sh</u>
9. _____the_____	16. _____Shop_____
10. _____	17. _____
11. _____	18. _____
12. _____	
13. _____	

Ends with <u>ng</u>	Ends with <u>sh</u>
14. _____	19. _____
15. _____	20. _____
	21. _____

Name _____ Date _____

Build Reading Fluency

When you read, pause between groups of words that go together.

Stan is in **/** a big rush. **//**

Stan has three minutes **/** to catch his plane. **//**

LISTEN AND LEARN TO READ

Listen to the story. When you hear a short pause, write a **/**.
When you hear a long pause, write **//**.

Rush!

Stan is in a big rush. His plane leaves at 2:00 p.m. The clock says 1:57 p.m. Stan has three minutes to catch his plane. That is not very long! He jumps out of the cab and slams the door. Bang! He drops his bag. All of his things fall out of the bag. Then he drops his ticket! A man helps Stan. He picks up the ticket and asks, "When does your plane leave?"

Stan says, "I think it just left without me."

The man looks at Stan's ticket. He grins and tells Stan, "You have enough time. Your plane leaves tomorrow at two."

PRACTICE

Now read the story to a partner. Read groups of words together.
Pause when you see a **/**.

Words to Know

READ AND WRITE

Read each word. Then write it.

1. people _____
2. come _____
3. by _____
4. animals _____
5. under _____
6. her _____
7. down _____
8. above _____
9. city _____
10. sometimes _____

WORD WORK

Read each sentence. Find the new words in the box.
Write the words on the lines.

11. This word is the opposite of **go**.

    ___come___

12. These 4 words are location words.

    _____   _____

    _____   _____

13. These 2 words name living things.

    _____   _____

14. These 2 words start with **c**.

    _____   _____

15. These 2 words end with **y**.

    _____   _____

16. This word has 2 smaller words in it.

    _____

17. These 2 words have **er**.

    _____   _____

18. This word rhymes with **my**.

    _____

Words with Short and Long Vowels

Name each picture. Read the two words. Circle the word
that names the picture.

1.

he / hen

2.

he / help

3.

hi / hit

4.

be / bell

Now read the story. Circle the words with long <u>e</u>.
Then circle the words with short <u>e</u>. Write them in
the chart. Write each word one time.

At Home in (the) City

    I like my home in the city. On
Saturdays, Sal and I help at the
library. He sits at the desk. I show
the kids good books. Then I let
them look around without me. At
12:00, we are done. Sometimes we
stop for lunch. Then we go home.
We walk down Grand Road. The
city is so great! We can be home
in two minutes.

Words with long <u>e</u>	Words with short <u>e</u>
5. ___the___	10. ___help___
6. _____	11. _____
7. _____	12. _____
8. _____	13. _____
9. _____	14. _____

Multisyllabic Words

Read each word. Write how many syllables it has.

1.

basket

2

2.

pumpkin

_____

3.

egg

_____

4.

muffin

_____

5.

stamp

_____

6.

plate

_____

7.

napkin

_____

8.

bench

_____

Now read the story. Circle the words with two syllables.
Write each word in the chart. Then write the syllables.

A (Picnic) in the Park

Jan and Chun go on a picnic. Jan
packs lunch in a basket. Chun grabs
a blanket. Then they put on their
helmets and hop on their bikes. They
ride through a tunnel, then up to
Elm Road. They watch out for traffic.
At the park, they see lots of children.
Chun puts the blanket on the grass,
and they sit down. "Let's eat," Jan
says. "Do you want a sandwich?"

	Word	Syllables	
9.	picnic	pic	nic
10.			
11.			
12.			
13.			
14.			
15.			
16.			

Build Reading Fluency

Some sentences tell something. Other sentences show strong feeling.

This sentence tells something. It ends with a **period.**

The rabbit is Velvet **.**

**This sentence shows a strong feeling.
It ends with an exclamation mark.**

He is so soft **!**

LISTEN AND LEARN TO READ

Listen to the different kinds of sentences.

Meet Jo

Jo works at the City Animal Hospital. I asked her to tell me about what she does at her job.

I have a great job. I love to help the animals. Look. This cat got hit in traffic. It is so sad when that happens. I had to make her a special bed.

This is Samson. Samson has a bad rash. He has this thing around his neck so he can't bite his skin. Sometimes we play catch. He needs to run a lot.

This rabbit is Velvet. I like to brush him. He is so soft! Velvet had to get his shots. He needs to rest for a day or two. Then he will go home.

So, that is my job. I help hundreds of animals. It is great to see them get well. I miss them when they go home.

PRACTICE

Now read the sentences to a partner.
See how your reading improves!

Words to Know

READ AND WRITE

Read each word. Then write it.

1. our _____	2. watch _____	3. family _____
4. eyes _____	5. father _____	6. really _____
7. head _____	8. mother _____	9. other _____
10. together _____		

WORD WORK

Read the clue. Write the word in the chart.
Then write the word again in the sentence.

What to Look For	Word	Sentence
11. means "dad"	f a t h e r	My _____father_____ is an artist.
12. means "mom"	_ _ _ _ _ _	My _____ is a writer.
13. begins with r	_ _ _ _ _ _	We have a _____ big family.
14. begins with to	_ _ _ _ _ _ _ _	We like to be _____.
15. ends with tch	_ _ _ _ _	Sometimes we _____ TV.
16. has her in it	_ _ _ _ _	We do _____ things, too.
17. has 3 letters	_ _ _	Friday is _____ game night.
18. has yes in it	_ _ _ _	I use my _____ to do puzzles.
19. rhymes with bed	_ _ _ _	I think with my _____.
20. begins with fam	_ _ _ _ _ _	My _____ loves games.

Name _____ Date _____

Words with Long Vowels

Name each picture. Write the name.

1.

cape

2.

_____

3.

_____

4.

_____

5.

_____

6.

_____

7.

_____

8.

_____

Now read the story. Circle the words with long <u>a</u>, <u>i</u>, <u>o</u>, or <u>u</u>. Write them in the chart. Write each word one time.

Fun with Bill

My brother Bill (drives) a truck
all around the state. When he is home,
he makes life fun.

Once he put together kites for
all the kids in the family. Bill had to
use long, thin tubes for the frames. The
wings were cloth from a torn robe.
"The kites are cute," he said, "but I
hope we can get them up in the air!"

9. _____	15. _____
10. _____	16. _____
11. _____	17. _____
12. drives	18. _____
13. _____	19. _____
14. _____	20. _____

Words with Long and Short Vowels

Name each picture. Read the two words. Circle the word that names the picture.

1.
(cap)/ cape

2.
pill / pile

3.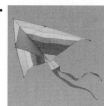
kit / kite

4.
tub / tube

5.
rob / robe

6.
cut / cute

7.
rod / rode

8.
tap / tape

Now read the story. Circle the words with long <u>o</u> or long <u>i</u>. Underline the words with short <u>o</u> or short <u>i</u>. Write them in the chart. Write each word one time.

A Busy (Home)

We are really busy. Here <u>is</u> what a day is like. Mom drives to the pet shop. She must be there by three. The shop closes at three. Then mom stops to get us snacks to eat. Dad helps me fix my bike, and then we scrub the stove. Pam has to watch the baby next door. At the end of the day, we like to sit down and rest. That is when we can all be together again.

9. __Home__	15. _____
10. _____	16. _____
11. _____	17. _____
12. _____	18. _____
13. _____	19. _____
14. _____	20. _____

COMPREHENSION

Build Reading Fluency

When you read, pause between groups of words that go together.

In Nicaragua, **/** my family made **/** big puppets to sell. **//**

We made the arms **/** from long tubes. **//**

LISTEN AND LEARN TO READ

**Listen to the story. When you hear a short pause, write a /.
When you hear a long pause, write //.**

Example: We made the arms **/** from long tubes. **//**

When We Came to Wisconsin

Hi. My name is Pablo Soto. My mother's name is Sandra. We are from Nicaragua.

In Nicaragua, my family made big puppets to sell. The name of one puppet that we made is La Gigantona. We made the head of this puppet with paper and paste. We made the eyes of the puppet really big, with long, thick lashes. We made the arms from long tubes. They swing from side to side. We put a white robe and a cute hat on the puppet. People like to watch this big puppet in parades.

PRACTICE

**Now read the story to a partner. Use the marks you
made to read groups of words together.**

HIGH FREQUENCY WORDS

Words to Know

READ AND WRITE

Read each word. Then write it.

1. once _____	2. world _____	3. below _____
4. or _____	5. river _____	6. water _____
7. places _____	8. always _____	9. through _____
10. important _____		

Find the new words. Write the words on the lines.

11. These 4 words have a **w**.

_____   _____

_____   _____

12. These 4 words have 1 syllable.

_____   _____

_____   _____

WORD WORK

Work with a partner. Follow the steps.

❶ Read aloud each new word in the box.

❷ Your partner writes the words.

❸ Have your partner read the words to you.

❹ Now you write the words on the lines below.

❺ Read the words to your partner.

13. _____	18. _____
14. _____	19. _____
15. _____	20. _____
16. _____	21. _____
17. _____	22. _____

Words with Long <u>a</u>, Long <u>e</u>, and Long <u>o</u>

Read each word. Which picture goes with the word? Write its letter.

1. coast <u>N</u>   2. boat ___   3. train ___   4. braid ___   5. road ___

6. seeds ___   7. paints ___   8. feet ___   9. sail ___   10. tree ___

11. tray ___   12. geese ___   13. crow ___   14. seal ___   15. tea ___

A.

B.

C.

D.

E.

F.

G.

H.

I.

J.

K.

L.

M.

N.

O.

Name each picture below. Which words above have the same long vowel sound as the picture name? Write the words on the lines.

16. train
___
___
___
___

17. ___
___
___
___
___

18. ___
___
___
___

WORD PATTERNS: *CVC, CVCC, CVVC*

Words with Short and Long Vowels

Name each picture. Read the two words. Circle the word that names the picture.

1.

cot / coat

2.

tap / tail

3.

bed / beach

4.

sell / seal

5.

pan / paint

6.

pens / peas

7.

cost / coast

8.

rod / road

Now read the story. Circle the words with long <u>a</u>. Underline the words with short <u>a</u>. Write them in the chart. Write each word one time.

Mom to the Rescue!

Nick (always) goes home to see his mom once a year. He <u>packs</u> his gray bag. What if it rains? Nick gets his coat. What if it's hot? Nick gets his swim trunks. He runs to catch the train, but he forgets his bag! Mom meets Nick in Bay City. She asks, "Where is your bag?" At home, Mom looks through the house. Nick waits. Mom comes back with his old clothes!

9. _always_	15. _packs_
10. _____	16. _____
11. _____	17. _____
12. _____	18. _____
13. _____	19. _____
14. _____	20. _____

Multisyllabic Words

Read each word. Write how many syllables it has.

1.
weekend
2
2.
crow
_____
3.
rowboat
_____
4.
train
_____

5.
coast
_____
6.
seashell
_____
7.
sunset
_____
8.
stream
_____

Now read the story. Circle the words with two syllables. Write each word in the chart one time. Then write the syllables.

At the (Seashore)

Dean goes to the seashore on weekends. On wet days, Dean wears his raincoat down to the beach. He hunts for seashells and digs for clams. On warm days, he stays on a sailboat with his dad. They sail from sunrise to sunset. Dean loves his weekends at the seashore.

Word	Syllables	
9. seashore	sea	shore
10. _____	_____	_____
11. _____	_____	_____
12. _____	_____	_____
13. _____	_____	_____
14. _____	_____	_____
15. _____	_____	_____

COMPREHENSION

Build Reading Fluency

When you read, pause between groups of words that go together.

Stay in your seat **/** while we move through the water. **//**

This is an important place **/** for animals, **/** too. **//**

LISTEN AND LEARN TO READ

Listen to the story. When you hear a short pause, write a **/** .

When you hear a long pause, write a **//** .

Example: This is an important place **/** for animals, **/** too. **//**

Explore a Wetland

Welcome to Black Creek Wetland. What a great way to spend a Sunday afternoon! My name is Jean Clay. I am your guide. Step into the rowboat. Stay in your seat while we move through the water.

Canada has many wetlands. Black Creek Wetland is one of them. A wetland is a low, wet place. Rainwater and many streams keep it wet. Black Creek is on the shore of Lake Ontario. Plants such as reeds and cattails grow here. This is an important place for animals, too. Ducks and geese lay their eggs here in May.

Sometimes, people drain the water from wetlands. Then they use the land to grow wheat or other crops. Not here. We plan to keep this wetland for the ducks, geese, and other animals.

PRACTICE

Now read the story to a partner. Read groups of words together. Make a short pause when you see a **/** . Make a long pause when you see a **//** .

Words to Know

READ AND WRITE

Read each word. Then write it.

1. saw _____	2. was _____	3. again _____
4. their _____	5. were _____	6. about _____
7. said _____	8. began _____	9. dance _____
10. thought _____		

WORD WORK

**Write the answer to each question. Find the new words
in the box. Write the words on the lines.**

11. Which 2 words start with **a**?

　　　_____again_____　　　_____about_____

12. Which 2 words have 3 letters?

　　　_____　　　_____

13. Which word rhymes with **red**?

　　　_____

14. Which word rhymes with **her**?

　　　_____

15. Which word means "started"?

　　　_____

16. Which word is the past tense of **think**?

　　　_____

17. Which word is the past tense of **see**?

　　　_____

18. Which 5 words have 5 letters each?

　　　_____　　　_____

　　　_____　　　_____

　　　_____

19. Which word means "once more"?

　　　_____

20. Which 3 words have 2 syllables?

　　　_____　　　_____

　　　_____

Verbs with -<u>ed</u>

Read each sentence. Change the word in dark type to tell about the past.

1. Lin and I ___planted___ seeds.
   (plant)

2. The next day it _____ on our seeds.
   (rain)

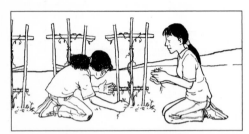

3. I _____ her pull the weeds.
   (help)

4. We _____ for the plants to grow.
   (wait)

5. We _____ a lot of peas.
   (pick)

6. We _____ them for our friends.
   (cook)

Now read the story. Circle the words with -<u>ed</u>. Write each word in the chart one time. Then write the root word.

We (Waited) for the Sun

On Saturday morning it rained . Kim and I waited for the sun. When it peeked through the clouds, we ran to the beach. We saw some birds and hunted for shells by the water. We cleaned the sand off the shells and put them in a box. Then we hunted for tiny crabs in the sand. Kim lifted one crab so we could see it up close.

Word with -<u>ed</u>	Root Word
7. Waited	wait
8. _____	_____
9. _____	_____
10. _____	_____
11. _____	_____
12. _____	_____

VERB ENDING: –ED

Verbs with -<u>ed</u>

Read each sentence. Change the word in dark type to tell about the past.

1. Lane and I ____planned____ a trip.
   (**plan**)

2. We _____ some snacks and water.
   (**grab**)

3. We _____ in the hills for six hours.
   (**hike**)

4. We laughed and _____ the whole time.
   (**joke**)

5. We _____ just before dark.
   (**stop**)

6. Later, we _____ to another friend about the trip.
   (**brag**)

Now read the story. Circle the words with -<u>ed</u>. Write each word in the chart one time. Then write the root word.

With a Friend

Ben's feet (dragged) as he jogged in the park. Sometimes he hated to jog by himself. He sat down on a bench to rest. Just then his friend Matt jogged by and waved.

"Matt!" Ben said. "Wait for me!" He hopped up and ran to catch up with Matt. He smiled as they ran side by side. It was more fun to jog with a friend!

Word with -<u>ed</u>	Root Word
7. ___dragged___	drag
8. _____	_____
9. _____	_____
10. _____	_____
11. _____	_____
12. _____	_____

Build Reading Fluency

When you read, pause between groups of words that go together.

She looked at the clock **/** above the stove. **//**

"Veronica has ten more seconds to get here," **/** she said. **//**

LISTEN AND LEARN TO READ

Listen to the story. When you hear a short pause, write a **/** .
When you hear a long pause, write **//** .

Example: "Veronica has ten more seconds to get here," **/** she said. **//**

Eva's Lesson

Eva was mad. She tapped her foot. She looked at the clock above the stove. "Veronica has ten more seconds to get here," she said. Eva waited and waited. Veronica was always late. They had planned to work on their dance for the school show. Eva thought Veronica was not very good. She thought Veronica needed a lot of help.

While she waited, Eva played the CD for their dance. She clapped her hands and kicked to the beat. She began to sing. She kicked again. This time, she kicked too high. She slipped and landed on the rug! Just then, Veronica peeked in the kitchen window. She saw Eva and rushed to help her. Eva smiled and rubbed her leg. "Now I know I was the one who needed help," she joked.

PRACTICE

Now read the story to a partner. Read groups of words together. Make a short pause when you see a **/** . Make a long pause when you see **//** .

HIGH FREQUENCY WORDS

Words to Know

READ AND WRITE

Read each word. Then write it.

1. celebrate _____
2. most _____
3. young _____
4. following _____
5. change _____
6. started _____
7. children _____
8. only _____
9. another _____
10. beginning _____

WORD WORK

Read each clue. Find the new words in the box.
Write the words on the lines.

11. This word starts with **f**.

   _____following_____

12. These 2 words begin with **ch**.

   _____

   _____

13. These 2 words have 4 letters each.

   _____

   _____

14. These words end with **e**.

   _____

   _____

15. These 2 words have **st**.

   _____

   _____

16. These 2 words end with **-ing**.

   _____

   _____

17. This word has the word **other** in it.

   _____

18. This word means "more than one child."

   _____

19. This word is the opposite of **old**.

   _____

20. This word is the opposite of **ended**.

   _____

VERB ENDING: -ING

Verbs with -ing

Read each sentence. Change the word in dark type to tell what is happening right now.

1. They are ____celebrating____ summer.
   (celebrate)

2. Some people are _____ trips.
   (take)

3. They are _____ in the pool.
   (swim)

4. They are _____ wet.
   (get)

5. This family is _____ outside.
   (sit)

6. They are _____ a picnic lunch.
   (eat)

Now read the story. Circle the words with -ing. Write each word in the chart one time. Then write the root word.

Our School Fair

Our school fair is (beginning) at 2 p.m. We are taking all the games outside. Suddenly, it is raining and we are beginning to get very wet. Most of us are rushing inside. Now we are waiting for the rain to stop. Yes. The sun is shining again. The fair can begin on time.

	Word with -ing	Root Word
7.	beginning	begin
8.		
9.		
10.		
11.		
12.		

Build Reading Fluency

Read the article. Stop when the timer goes off. Mark your score. Then try it again two more times on different days.

Celebrate the 4th of July

America's birthday is the 4th of July. It is a time to celebrate. You can have a picnic in the park or watch a parade. Hundreds of people stand on the street and wait for the parade to begin. The school bands are first. You can feel the drums. Next are the fire trucks with wailing sirens. Then the floats pass by. Boys and girls clap and yell. They wave red, white, and blue flags.

Celebrating brings people together. They all come to have a good time. Old people and young children dance in the streets. Kids eat hot dogs and corn on the cob. They smile as their dads take pictures. This is the best way to celebrate the 4th of July!

	Day 1	Day 2	Day 3
Total Words Read in One Minute	____	____	____
Minus Words Missed	____	____	____
Words Read Correctly in One Minute	____	____	____

Words to Know

READ AND WRITE

Read each word. Then write it.

1. life _____	2. been _____	3. sound _____
4. four _____	5. almost _____	6. caused _____
7. often _____	8. never _____	9. could _____
10. between _____		

Answer each question.

11. Which words start with **c**?

_____ _____

12. Which words have the letters **ee** together?

_____ _____

WORD WORK

Read each sentence. Choose a word from the box above.
Then write it in the sentence.

13. My little brother is _____four_____ years old.

14. Kento has been lost only once in his _____ .

15. He _____ always holds Mom's hand.

16. One day Mom said he _____ walk without her.

17. He has always _____ fast, and he ran from her.

18. A clerk heard a _____ .

19. She _____ helps lost children.

20. Kento _____ Mom a lot of worry.

21. He _____ runs from her now.

22. He stays _____ Mom and me!

Name _____   Date _____

Words with Long i or Long u

Name each picture. Write the name.

1.

___pie___

2.

_____

3.

_____

4.

_____

5.
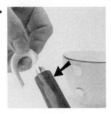
_____

6.

_____

Now read the story. Circle the words with long i or long u.
Write them in the chart. Write each word one time.

The (Right) Thing

Nam often helps at the senior
center. He thinks it's the right thing
to do. He helps in many ways. He
serves pie. He brings in books and
takes back the books that are (due.) In
art class, Nam helps people cut and
glue things. He gets the paints—
bright red, yellow, blue. Four nights a
year, the center has a big show. Nam
wears a suit and tie. The shows are
always great!

7. ___right___	12. ___due___
8. _____	13. _____
9. _____	14. _____
10. _____	15. _____
11. _____	

75

Build Reading Fluency

Read the article. Stop when the timer goes off. Mark your
score. Then try it again two more times on different days.

First-Aid Class

I went to a first-aid class at school. I learned the right
way to treat cuts and sprains and other injuries. I thought
the class was a lot of fun.

Then, last week, Tom and I went bike riding. Tom fell
off his bike and got a cut over his eye. He sprained his
right foot, too. The first thing I did was call his mom. I
asked her to bring some ice. Then I got the first-aid kit
from my backpack. I cleaned up Tom's cut and put a
band-aid over it. His foot started to swell. I wrapped it
with a strip of elastic bandage, but made sure it wasn't
too tight!

Tom was very impressed. "You should be a doctor!"
he said.

The first-aid class was fun, but I never dreamed it was
so important. Some things are really good to know.

	Day 1	Day 2	Day 3
Total Words Read in One Minute	_____	_____	_____
Minus Words Missed	_____	_____	_____
Words Read Correctly in One Minute	_____	_____	_____

Words to Know

READ AND WRITE

Read each word. Then write it.

1. now _____	2. would _____	3. also _____
4. called _____	5. should _____	6. know _____
7. lived _____	8. house _____	9. country _____
10. American _____		

WORD WORK

Read each sentence. Find the new words in the box.
Write the words on the lines.

11. These 2 words rhyme.

_____would_____   _____should_____

12. This word is the opposite of **later**.

_____

13. This word rhymes with **show**.

_____

14. This word rhymes with **cow**.

_____

15. This word has the word **so** in it.

_____

16. This word means almost the same
as **home**.

_____

17. These 2 words are past tense verbs.

_____   _____

18. This word always begins with a
capital letter.

_____

19. These 2 words have a silent **l**.

_____   _____

20. These 2 words have 2 syllables.

_____   _____

Words with R-controlled Vowels

Name each picture. Write the name.

1.

car

2.

_____

3.

_____

4.

_____

5.

_____

6.

_____

7.

_____

8.

_____

Now read the story. Circle the words that go in the chart. Write them in the chart. Write each word one time.

(Part) of a Team

Melvin is part of a rescue team. When sea birds are hurt after a storm or an oil spill, his team takes them to a yard. First they clean off the oil and dirt. Melvin holds the birds and turns them as he washes off the oil. He stays at the yard from morning until night. It is a hard job, but it is important. When the birds chirp in a happy way, Melvin is also happy. He knows that the birds may survive.

9. _____part_____ 10. _____ 11. _____	16. _____ 17. _____ 18. _____ 19. _____

12. _____ 13. _____ 14. _____ 15. _____	20. _____ 21. _____ 22. _____

Words with R-controlled Vowels

Name each picture. Write the name.

1.

steer

2.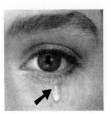

_____

3.

_____

4.

_____

5.

_____

6.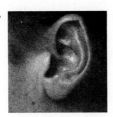

_____

7.

_____

8.

_____

Now read the story. Circle the words that go in the chart.
Write them in the chart.

A Great Guy

Lee always (cheers) people up. One year, when I was sick, he gave me a toy deer. It was so funny. It had a wig with long hair and a pair of sunglasses. Last year, Lee planted tomatoes near his house. He gave my mom a bag of big, bright tomatoes. Lee also helps a family in another country. He sends them socks to wear. He brings stuffed bears to kids in Children's Hospital.

9. cheers	13. _____
10. _____	14. _____
11. _____	15. _____
12. _____	16. _____

Build Reading Fluency

Read the article. Stop when the timer goes off. Mark your score.
Then try it again two more times on different days.

Another Kid Helps Kids

Kimmie Weeks started making a difference when he was 10. The year was 1991. His country, Liberia, was at war. Many homes and schools were destroyed. Hundreds of children had no food. Many were sick. The fighting was so bad, children were trained to be soldiers. No one seemed to know what to do. Kimmie felt he had to help.

He and other kids started cleaning the streets. They picked up bricks, stones, and other trash left after the fighting. Then he started speaking on the radio. He said that children should not fight in war. His speeches helped. In 1996, Liberia stopped training children to fight.

Kimmie is now a young man. He is still helping the children of his country. He raises money to open more schools. Today, many children have better lives thanks to Kimmie Weeks.

	Day 1	Day 2	Day 3
Total Words Read in One Minute	_____	_____	_____
Minus Words Missed	_____	_____	_____
Words Read Correctly in One Minute	_____	_____	_____

Words to Know

READ AND WRITE

Read each word. Then write it.

1. story _____	2. oil _____	3. why _____
4. found _____	5. over _____	6. try _____
7. because _____	8. away _____	9. few _____
10. mountains _____		

Answer each question.

11. Which words begin with the letter **f**?

_____ _____

12. Which words rhyme with **by**?

_____ _____

WORD WORK

Work with a partner. Follow the steps.

1 Read aloud each new word in the box.

2 Your partner writes the words.

3 Have your partner read the words to you.

4 Now you write the words on the lines below.

5 Read the words to your partner.

13. _____   18. _____

14. _____   19. _____

15. _____   20. _____

16. _____   21. _____

17. _____   22. _____

Types of Syllables

Name each picture. Read the two words.
Circle the word that names the picture.

1.
marker / (market)

2.
letter / winter

3.
perfume / person

4.
under / ladder

5.
garden / garter

6.
timber / corner

7.
hammer / summer

8.
butter / pepper

Now read the story. Then read each word in the chart.
Write the syllables in the word.

My Sister Meg

My sister Meg should live on a farm and drive a tractor. She loves to grow things! She gets perfect seeds at the market and plants them in our garden. She plants peppers for Dad and turnips for Mom. Gram asks for butter beans. Meg plants a few things for herself: plums and peas. We all help harvest what she grows. Then we cook supper. Food from the garden always tastes better!

Words	Syllables	
9. sister	sis	ter
10. perfect	___	___
11. garden	___	___
12. peppers	___	___
13. turnips	___	___
14. butter	___	___
15. harvest	___	___
16. supper	___	___

Build Reading Fluency

**Read the article. Stop when the timer goes off. Mark your score.
Then try it again two more times on different days.**

A Robin's Nest

The American robin is the biggest member of the thrush family. It is not hard to spot a robin. It is gray with a black head. The throat is white with black streaks. The chest is an orange-red.

After winter, most birds make new nests. Many birds use twigs and leaves to make their nests. A robin uses twigs, leaves, spring grasses, and mud. They use the mud to make the nest strong. Then they line the nest with grass. The grass makes the nest soft and warm for the eggs. A robin lays four or five eggs each spring. The eggs are light blue without any spots.

Robins are quite at home living near people, so you may find their nests in parks or gardens. Look for them in spring!

	Day 1	Day 2	Day 3
Total Words Read in One Minute	_____	_____	_____
Minus Words Missed	_____	_____	_____
Words Read Correctly in One Minute	_____	_____	_____

Words to Know

READ AND WRITE

Read each word. Then write it.

1. words _____	2. back _____	3. example _____
4. ever _____	5. miss _____	6. along _____
7. much _____	8. news _____	9. before _____
10. question _____		

WORD WORK

Read the clue. Write the word in the chart.
Then write the word again in the sentence.

What to Look For	Word	Sentence
11. ends with **ss**	m i s s	I ___miss___ my friend.
12. has a **v**	_ _ _ _	He's the best friend I _____ had.
13. means "a lot"	_ _ _ _	I like him so _____.
14. has an **x**	_ _ _ _ _ _ _	Ted is an _____ of a true friend.
15. tells when	_ _ _ _ _ _	He left _____ summer.
16. ends with **ng**	_ _ _ _ _	I went _____ to say good-bye.
17. has **ew**	_ _ _ _	Now I send Ted my _____.
18. begins with **w**	_ _ _ _ _	I write lots of _____.
19. ends with **tion**	_ _ _ _ _ _ _ _	I ask him one _____.
20. ends with **ck**	_ _ _ _	When will you come _____?

Words with <u>y</u>

Read each word. Tell if the letter <u>y</u> is a vowel or a consonant.

1.

yard

consonant _____

2.

twenty

_____

3.

sky

_____

4.

happy

_____

5.

year

_____

6.

yarn

_____

Read the story. Circle the words with <u>y</u>. Write the words in the chart. Write each word one time.

(Why) **I Admire Raoul Wallenburg**

    My class read about World War II. In one (story,) a man risked his life to save others. He could not be happy while other people suffered so much. He gave a lot of lucky people passports so that they could escape. He helped other people find places to hide. By the end of the war, he had helped 100,000 people.

7. ___Why___	10. ___story___
8. _____	11. _____
9. _____	12. _____

WORDS WITH Y

Plurals: y + s, y to i + es

Read each sentence. Change the word in dark type to name more than one.

1. I have many ____hobbies____ .
   (**hobby**)

2. On some _____ , I make model planes from
   (**day**)
   World War II.

3. My _____ like to help me.
   (**buddy**)

4. We eat lunch on _____ as we work.
   (**tray**)

5. We tell each other _____ about the planes.
   (**story**)

6. We pretend the planes are still up in the _____ .
   (**sky**)

Now read the story. Circle the plurals that end in -ys and -ies.
Write each word in the chart. Then write the root word.

Dad's Favorite Hobby

  My dad has many (hobbies.) The hobby
he likes best is history. He likes to read
about England and other countries in
World War II. Sometimes he tells me
stories about those days. Dad has other
ways to learn about history. For example,
he collects old things, like newspapers,
stamps, and coins from the forties.

Word that Ends in -ys or -ies	Root Word
7. ____hobbies____	____hobby____
8. _____	_____
9. _____	_____
10. _____	_____
11. _____	_____
12. _____	_____

Build Reading Fluency

Read the letter. Stop when the timer goes off. Mark your score.
Then try it again two more times on different days.

> June 25, 1937
> Oshkosh, Wisconsin
>
> Dear Sister,
>
>   Thank you for the letter. I love reading the news from Poland.
>
>   Well, my first year in America has not been easy. This is a fine country, but I was not always happy. It was hard to find a job. I had no money for a long time. Uncle Jedrick paid for the things I needed. Today my life is much better! I work six days a week in a factory. Now I can help Uncle Jedrick pay for food. I am also saving a few pennies each week. This summer I will have money to send to Mom.
>
>   I miss you so much! I wait for the day you and Mom can come to America. Then we will all be together again! Until then, think of me and write often!
>
>   Love,
>   Konrad

	Day 1	Day 2	Day 3
Total Words Read in One Minute	_____	_____	_____
Minus Words Missed	_____	_____	_____
Words Read Correctly in One Minute	_____	_____	_____

Words to Know

READ AND WRITE

Read each word. Then write it.

1. each _____	2. sentence _____	3. as _____
4. idea _____	5. plants _____	6. into _____
7. made _____	8. seemed _____	9. but _____
10. until _____		

WORD WORK

Read each sentence. Find the new words in the box.
Write the words on the lines.

11. These 2 words start with **s**.

    <u>sentence</u>   <u>seemed</u>

12. This word is the first in ABC order.

_____

13. These 2 words have **ea**.

_____ _____

14. This word names things that grow.

_____

15. These 2 words have a **u**.

_____ _____

16. These 4 words have 4 letters each.

_____ _____

_____ _____

17. This word is the last in ABC order.

_____

18. This word is the opposite of **out of**.

_____

19. These 2 words have an **m**.

_____ _____

20. These 2 words are things you write.

_____ _____

DIPHTHONGS

Words with <u>oi</u>, <u>oy</u>, <u>ou</u>, and <u>ow</u>

Read each word. Which picture goes with the word? Write its letter.

1. boil   *G*   2. couch ___   3. owl ___   4. crown ___   5. house ___

6. cloud ___   7. boy ___   8. crowd ___   9. coin ___   10. points ___

11. proud ___   12. soil ___   13. mouse ___   14. frown ___   15. toys ___

A.  B.  C.  D.  E.

F.  G.  H.  I.  J.

K.  L.  M.  N.  O.

Read each word. Find the word or words above that have the same vowel sound *and* spelling. Write the words on the lines.

16. join   17. joy   18. loud   19. clown

   boil

VARIANT VOWELS

Words with <u>oo</u>, <u>ew</u>, <u>au</u>, <u>aw</u>, <u>al</u>, and <u>all</u>

Read each word. Which picture goes with the word? Write its letter.

1. mall H   2. saw __   3. broom __   4. salt __   5. screw __

6. hawk __   7. author __   8. moon __   9. stew __   10. hall __

11. draw __   12. boots __   13. laundry __   14. pool __   15. ball __

A.    B.    C.    D.    E.

F.    G.    H.    I.    J.

K. 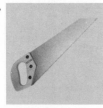   L.    M.    N.    O.

Read each word. Find the words above that have the same
sound *and* spelling. Write the words on the lines.

16. cool ___broom___   17. awful _____   18. small _____

_____   _____   _____

_____   _____   _____

_____

19. chew _____   20. haunted _____   21. also _____

_____   _____

Build Reading Fluency

Read the story. Stop when the timer goes off. Mark your score. Then try it again two more times on different days.

Storyteller

Paul Brown peeked into the hospital room. He saw Maddie staring out the window. She seemed bored.

Paul said, "Hi," as he walked in.

"Hi," Maddie answered. "Who are you?"

"I'm your storyteller."

Maddie frowned. "Wrong room," she said. "I'm too old for stories."

"How old are you?" Paul asked.

"Thirteen," Maddie answered.

"Perfect!" said Paul. Before Maddie could object, he began to tell a story.

Paul was a fine storyteller. He changed the sound of his voice for each character. He made it high like a girl, low like a man, or into a deep growl like a bear. He changed his shape and the way he moved, too. He turned himself into each character.

Soon Maddie was laughing out loud. "Who are you?" she asked again.

Paul bowed. "I am you. I am me. I am every person. I am a storyteller."

	Day 1	Day 2	Day 3
Total Words Read in One Minute	_____	_____	_____
Minus Words Missed	_____	_____	_____
Words Read Correctly in One Minute	_____	_____	_____

Words to Know

READ AND WRITE

Read each word. Then write it.

1. talked _____	2. asked _____	3. if _____
4. walked _____	5. while _____	6. such _____
7. trees _____	8. even _____	9. air _____
10. friends _____		

Answer each question.

11. Which words have 4 letters?

_____ _____

12. Which words rhyme?

_____ _____

WORD WORK

Work with a partner. Follow the steps.

1 Read aloud each new word in the box.

2 Your partner writes the words.

3 Have your partner read the words to you.

4 Now you write the words on the lines below.

5 Read the words to your partner.

13. _____   18. _____

14. _____   19. _____

15. _____   20. _____

16. _____   21. _____

17. _____   22. _____

Name _____ Date _____

Words with Hard and Soft c or g

Read each word. Find the picture that goes with the word. Write its letter.

1. gum L
2. garden ___
3. gem ___
4. race ___

5. city ___
6. goat ___
7. cones ___
8. cent ___

9. gate ___
10. cut ___
11. pages ___
12. cap ___

A.
B.
C.
D.

E.
F.
G.
H.

I.
J.
K.
L.

Name each picture below. Find the word or words in which the c or g makes the same sound. Write the words on the lines.

13. cones
_____

14. _____
_____

15. _____
_____
_____

16. _____
_____

Words with /ŏŏ/ or Silent Consonants

Name each picture. Write the name.

1.
cookies

2.
_____

3.
_____

4.
_____

5.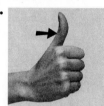
_____

6.
_____

7.
_____

8.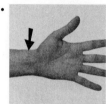
_____

Now read the story. Circle the words with /ŏŏ/ or silent consonants. Write them in the chart. Write each word one time.

My Very Best

I love to play football. I was a good player, but Coach said, "I know you can do better." So one day I walked to the library to get a book about football. I stood in the sports section a long time and looked at many books. Finally, I took one that had lots of tips: how to dodge other players, throw, and even how to keep your knees from getting wrecked. Thanks to that book, I don't do anything wrong now. Coach and my friends give me the thumbs up!

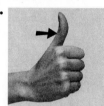	
9. ___football___	15. ___know___
10. _____	16. _____
11. _____	17. _____
12. _____	18. _____
13. _____	19. _____
14. _____	20. _____

Build Reading Fluency

Read the article. Stop when the timer goes off. Mark your score.
Then try it again two more times on different days.

Hard Ice

Ice is hard. When you fall on ice, you really feel it.
My name is Sonny Chen. I'm an ice skater, so I know
what I'm talking about. I started skating when I was
three years old. Back then, I spent more time falling on
the ice than skating. Yet I loved the sport even then.

When I was ten, I learned a move called "the axel."
To do this move, I go forward on the outside edge of one
skate. After gaining speed, I leap off the ice and spin
in the air. I land on the outside edge of the other skate.
It took me a long time to get it right the first time.
Then, suddenly, I nailed it! I made a perfect landing! What
a great feeling that was. It was worth ten thousand falls,
even on hard ice.

	Day 1	Day 2	Day 3
Total Words Read in One Minute	_____	_____	_____
Minus Words Missed	_____	_____	_____
Words Read Correctly in One Minute	_____	_____	_____

HIGH FREQUENCY WORDS

Words to Know

READ AND WRITE

Read each word. Then write it.

1. earth _____	2. state _____	3. form _____
4. million _____	5. than _____	6. sea _____
7. miles _____	8. near _____	9. high _____
10. explore _____		

Answer each question.

11. Which words have two syllables?

_____ _____

12. Which words have **th**?

_____ _____

WORD WORK

Read each sentence. Choose a word from the box above.
Then write it in the sentence.

13. Caves are hollow places in the ____earth____ .

14. They are found inland and by the _____ .

15. Some caves are bigger _____ others.

16. Mammoth Cave is in the _____ of Kentucky.

17. It is _____ the city of Bowling Green.

18. The cave is under a _____ ridge of limestone.

19. It is over 340 _____ long.

20. Rivers under the ground _____ lakes inside the cave.

21. Mammoth Cave is over one _____ years old.

22. People like to _____ Mammoth Cave.

Mammoth Cave

Name _____ Date _____

Multisyllabic Words

Read each word. Write how many syllables it has.

1.

crown
_____1_____

2.

cactus
_____

3.

fifty
_____

4.

salt
_____

5.

badge
_____

6.

children
_____

7.

tray
_____

8.

hundred
_____

Now read the story. Circle the words with two syllables. Write each word in the chart. Then write the syllables in the word. Write each word one time.

The Old Days

My class went to a (hamlet) near Boston. A hamlet is a small town. We learned how children and their folks lived in the past. In the hamlet, actors dress in costumes and do things by hand. We watched a girl in a long dress churn butter. We saw a man make nails. Life was hard hundreds of years ago. When we got back to school, we had a contest to see who knew the most facts.

	Word	Syllables	
9.	hamlet	ham	let
10.			
11.			
12.			
13.			
14.			
15.			
16.			

Multisyllabic Words

Read each word. Write how many syllables it has.

1.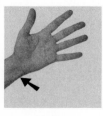
music

2.
wagon

3.
knife

4.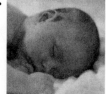
stage

2

5.
wrist

6.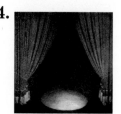
planet

7.
city

8.
asleep

Now read the story. Then read each word in the chart.
Write the syllables in the word.

Niagara Falls

Niagara Falls is near Buffalo, New
York. Last week, my mom and I went
to visit the falls. We stayed in a cozy
cabin. We rode up the river in a boat.
The waterfalls amazed me. The roar of
the falls is so loud! The falls are about
175 feet high. They formed about
12,000 years ago. Next time, you should
come along!

Words	Syllables	
9. visit	vis	it
10. cozy		
11. cabin		
12. about		
13. ago		
14. along		

Build Reading Fluency

Read the article. Stop when the timer goes off. Mark your score.
Then try it again two more times on different days.

The Pony Express Trail

Before 1860, it took three weeks to carry mail across the United States. It traveled slowly by boat and by stage coach. Then the U.S. started a new mail service. It was called the Pony Express. Many boys worked for the Pony Express. They rode fast ponies between the state of Missouri and the California coast. Each rider rode about 75 miles, changing ponies along the way. After 75 miles, another rider would take the mailbag. The riders rode day and night. They rode through heat, rain, and snow. They traveled 1,966 miles across plains, deserts, and high mountains. The entire trip took ten days. The riders were paid $100 to $150 a month. That was a lot of money in 1860, and the riders earned every penny of it.

	Day 1	Day 2	Day 3
Total Words Read in One Minute	_____	_____	_____
Minus Words Missed	_____	_____	_____
Words Read Correctly in One Minute	_____	_____	_____

Words to Know

READ AND WRITE

Read each word. Then write it.

1. healthy _____	2. weigh _____	3. cold _____
4. outdoors _____	5. indoors _____	6. warm _____
7. special _____	8. own _____	9. any _____
10. beautiful _____		

WORD WORK

Read the clue. Write the word in the chart.
Then write the word again in the sentence.

What to Look For	Word	Sentence
11. starts with **sp**	s p e c i a l	Fall is a ___special___ time.
12. means "outside"	_ _ _ _ _ _ _ _	I work _____ under the sky.
13. means "belongs to me"	_ _ _	I want my _____ garden.
14. ends with **-ful**	_ _ _ _ _ _ _ _ _	My berries are _____.
15. is the opposite of **cool**	_ _ _ _	They love the _____ sun.
16. means "not sick"	_ _ _ _ _ _ _	The pumpkins are _____, too.
17. rhymes with **say**	_ _ _ _ _	They can _____ 20 pounds.
18. is the opposite of **hot**	_ _ _ _	Today is windy and _____.
19. rhymes with **many**	_ _ _	There isn't _____ sun.
20. means "inside"	_ _ _ _ _ _ _	So I stay _____ and read.

SUFFIXES

Suffixes: -<u>ly</u>, -<u>y</u>

The suffix -<u>ly</u> changes an adjective to an adverb. The suffix -<u>y</u> changes a noun to an adjective. Read each sentence. Add -<u>ly</u> or -<u>y</u> to the word in dark type to complete the sentence.

1.

The sun is **bright**. It shines _____brightly_____ .

2.

The drums are **loud**. The boy plays _____ .

3.

This room is a **mess**. It is _____messy_____ .

4.

The machine digs up **dirt**. It gets _____ .

5.

He is a **safe** rider. He rides _____ .

6.

The boy plays in the **sand**. He gets _____ .

Now read the story. Circle each word with the suffix -<u>ly</u> or -<u>y</u> . Write the words in the chart. Then write the root words.

In the Garden

Kim's alarm clock rang loudly. She still felt sleepy! She dressed quickly in old pants and tiptoed softly into the garden. It was a warm, windy day. Kim bent down and dug in the rocky soil. Suddenly her hand hit something. She dug a little more and discovered a big, brown potato. Kim pulled it out of the dirt. "It must weigh five pounds," she thought. "It could make a healthy meal for six people."

Word with -<u>ly</u>	Root Word
7. _____loudly_____	_____loud_____
8. _____	_____
9. _____	_____
10. _____	_____

Word with -<u>y</u>	Root Word
11. _____	_____
12. _____	_____
13. _____	_____
14. _____	_____

SUFFIXES

Suffixes: -<u>ful</u>, -<u>less</u>

The suffix -<u>ful</u> means "full of." The suffix -<u>less</u> means "without." Add -<u>ful</u> or -<u>less</u> to each word to make a new word. Write the word that goes with each picture.

1.  end<u>less</u>

2.  fear_____

3.  use_____

4.  peace<u>ful</u>

5. grace_____

6.  harm_____

Now read the story. Circle each word with the suffix -<u>ful</u> or -<u>less</u>. Write the words in the chart. Then write the root words.

Sun and Wind

Mike looked at his grape vines. The hot sun beat down on the plants. A warm wind began to blow. Mike was worried because wind can be (harmful) to grapes. The wind blew for days. It seemed endless. "I hope my vines survive," Mike thought. "I wish I could do something, but I am helpless." He felt so useless. At last, the wind stopped. It was peaceful again. The grape vines still looked healthy. Mike felt very thankful.

Word with -<u>ful</u>	Root Word
7. _____harmful_____	_____harm_____
8. _____	_____
9. _____	_____

Word with -<u>less</u>	Root Word
10. _____	_____
11. _____	_____
12. _____	_____

Prefixes: <u>re-</u>, <u>un-</u>

The prefix <u>re-</u> can mean "again." The prefix <u>un-</u> can mean "not" or "the opposite of." Add <u>re-</u> or <u>un-</u> to each word to make a new word. Write the word that goes with the picture.

1.  __re__build

2.  ____write

3.  ____place

4.  __un__lock

5.  ____happy

6.  ____cut

Now read the story. Circle each word with the prefix <u>re-</u> or <u>un-</u>. Write the words in the chart. Then write the root words.

Miller's Farm

At Miller's Farm you can (relive) the past. You can taste fresh, unsalted peanuts. You can also make your own peanut butter. First, untie a big sack and take some peanuts. Be sure to retie the sack. Take off the shells, then put the peanuts in a grinder. Grind the peanuts to make peanut butter. Uncover a jar and fill it. Put the cover on the jar. Refill the grinder to make more peanut butter.

Word with <u>re-</u>	Root Word
7. ____relive____	live
8. _____	_____
9. _____	_____

Word with <u>un-</u>	Root Word
10. _____	_____
11. _____	_____
12. _____	_____

Build Reading Fluency

Read the article. Stop when the timer goes off. Mark your score.
Then try it again two more times on different days.

Farmers' Market

It is 5 a.m. A pickup truck drives slowly into a parking lot. A farmer quickly sets up a table outdoors. She unloads freshly picked fruit and healthy green beans. Another driver unloads crusty rolls and tasty pies. Suddenly the lot fills with trucks.

Shoppers are eagerly arriving now. Farmers quickly untie bags of corn and stack up endless piles of crunchy nuts. They display jars of wonderful homemade jams. Some farmers proudly offer free samples. Lucky shoppers taste the tomatoes. They are really flavorful—unlike the tasteless tomatoes you find in some stores.

At 4 p.m., the farmers reload their trucks. The lot is silent again. Tomorrow, it may be warm, cold, rainy, or windy. No matter what the weather may be, the farmers' market will reopen tomorrow in another town.

	Day 1	Day 2	Day 3
Total Words Read in One Minute	_____	_____	_____
Minus Words Missed	_____	_____	_____
Words Read Correctly in One Minute	_____	_____	_____

Words to Know

READ AND WRITE

Read each word. Then write it.

1. right _____   2. close _____   3. show _____

4. watch _____   5. kind _____

Answer each question.

6. Which 3 words name actions?

_____   _____

_____

7. Which 2 words also name things?

_____   _____

WORD WORK

Read each question. Find the new words in the box.
Write the words on the lines.

8. Which word is the opposite of **left**?

_____

9. Which 2 words can be both a
verb and a noun?

_____   _____

10. Which word means "near"?

_____

11. Which 2 words can be adjectives?

_____   _____

12. Which word is the opposite of **hide**?

_____

13. Which word means "type of"?

_____

14. Which word is the opposite of **open**?

_____

15. Which word means "look at"?

_____

MULTISYLLABIC WORDS

Types of Syllables

Name each picture. Read the two words.
Circle the word that names the picture.

1.

middle / (pickle)

2.

table / little

3.

circle / gentle

4.

beetle / eagle

5.

apple / able

6.

candle / huddle

7.

twinkle / title

8.

turtle / purple

Now read the story. Circle the words with a consonant + <u>le</u>.
Write them in the chart.

A Native American (Fable)

Native Americans tell stories about
Coyote. In one story, Coyote sees a (little)
star that twinkles like a candle. "Come
close!" Coyote yells. "I want to dance with
you." The star floats down and he grabs it.
He soars like an eagle, high over Table
Rock. He isn't able to hang on. His hands
slip and he tumbles down. Splat! He lands
by a beetle. What did Coyote learn? It's
simple: You can't do everything you want.

Long Vowel in First Syllable	Short Vowel in First Syllable
9. ___Fable___	14. ___little___
10. _____	15. _____
11. _____	16. _____
12. _____	17. _____
13. _____	18. _____

Types of Syllables

**Name each picture. Read the two words. Circle the word
that names the picture.**

1.

(telescope) / tolerate

2.

fourteen / fifteen

3.

reptile / record

4.

aboard / alone

5.

beneath / between

6.

remain / repeat

7.

fearful / faithful

8.

celebrate / calculate

**Now read the story. Circle the two-syllable words.
Find the vowel pattern. Write each word in the chart.
Write each word one time.**

Apollo (Thirteen)

In 1970, a space (capsule) tried to reach the
moon. However, a mistake caused two air tanks
to explode. No one knew the reason for the
mistake. Yet the craft could not go to the moon.
The astronauts had to survive, so they released
the tanks. Teams on Earth watched and helped
the crew succeed. They exclaimed joyfully
when the astronauts got home alive.

Two Vowels Work Together	Vowel and <u>e</u> Work Together
9. _Thirteen_	14. _capsule_
10. _____	15. _____
11. _____	16. _____
12. _____	17. _____
13. _____	18. _____

Multisyllabic Words

Read each word. Write how many syllables it has.

1.

eagle

2

2.

unbuckle

_____

3.

faithful

_____

4.

superstar

_____

5.
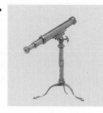
telescope

_____

6.

replace

_____

7.

candle

_____

8.

unafraid

_____

Now read the story. Circle the words with more than one syllable. Write each word in the chart one time. Then write the syllables in the word.

The (Republic) of Blues

My band is called The Republic of Blues. A lot of faithful fans come to our shows. They love our kind of music. I play the steel drums and Clive sings. He likes to rearrange old songs, too. I like his simple love songs best. I hope he does not leave the band. I would be so unhappy. I don't think I could replace him. I hope we will both be stars one day!

Word	Syllables		
9. Republic	Re	pub	lic
10. _____	____	____	
11. _____	____	____	
12. _____	____	____	
13. _____	____	____	
14. _____	____	____	
15. _____	____	____	

Build Reading Fluency

Read the myth. Stop when the timer goes off. Mark your score. Then try it again two more times on different days.

A Tale from Greece

When the sun is very hot, the people of Greece remember an old tale. It is about an inventor named Daedalus. The king was angry with Daedalus because he helped destroy the king's monster bull. The king punished him by locking him and his son Icarus inside a high tower.

Daedalus planned a clever escape. He plucked feathers from birds that visited the tower. He used candle wax to glue the feathers onto wooden frames. In this way, he made two pairs of wings.

When they put on the wings, Daedalus told Icarus, "Promise me you will not fly too high. If you do, the sun will melt the wax."

Icarus nodded, but when he flew into the sky, the boy forgot his promise. He flew higher and higher. Daedalus called out, but his cry came too late. The boy's wings melted, and he fell into the sea.

	Day 1	Day 2	Day 3
Total Words Read in One Minute	_____	_____	_____
Minus Words Missed	_____	_____	_____
Words Read Correctly in One Minute	_____	_____	_____

Timed Reading Chart

How many words did you read correctly for each selection?
Complete the chart to show your scores for each day.

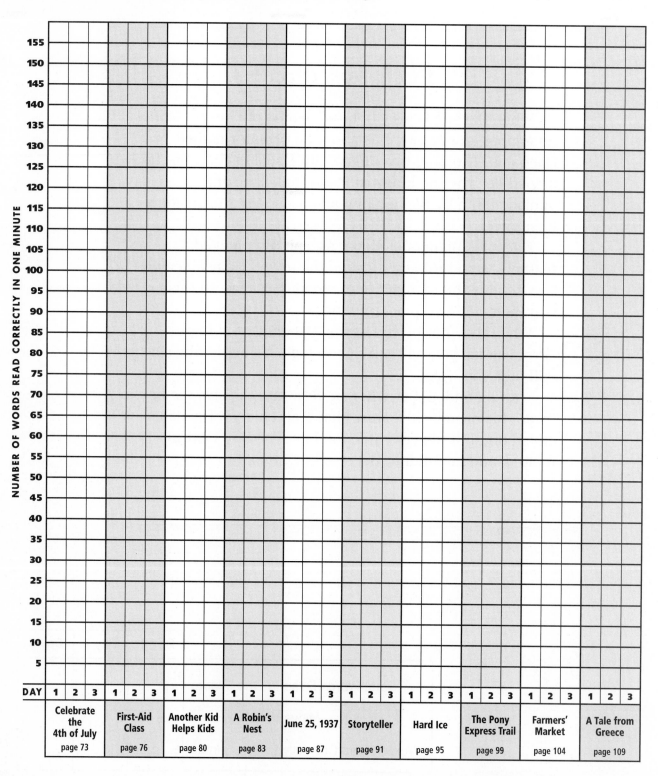

NUMBER OF WORDS READ CORRECTLY IN ONE MINUTE

DAY	1	2	3	1	2	3	1	2	3	1	2	3	1	2	3	1	2	3	1	2	3	1	2	3	1	2	3	1	2	3

Celebrate the 4th of July page 73	First-Aid Class page 76	Another Kid Helps Kids page 80	A Robin's Nest page 83	June 25, 1937 page 87	Storyteller page 91	Hard Ice page 95	The Pony Express Trail page 99	Farmers' Market page 104	A Tale from Greece page 109

Decodable Stories

A City Food Festival

We can't stop yet!

You go. I can't move. No more food festivals for me.

Look Back at A City Food Festival

CHECK YOUR UNDERSTANDING

1. Where do Pedro and Ekram go?

2. What do they do there?

3. How does the story end?

WORD WORK: Multisyllabic Words

Find these words in the story.

happens	hundreds
basket	napkin
pumpkin	sandwich

Circle the words. Then write the syllables in each word.

happens   hap pens

This is Pedro's first time at a food festival.

Have a basket of fish and chips. They are great!

Look at all the food stands, Ekram!

The boys are still hungry! They see a man with muffins to sell.

Me, too. I like pumpkin muffins.

I want a muffin.

At Home

Long Vowels: *a, i, o, u*

Grandmother likes all the things we do for her. She even likes my brother's drums.

CRASH!

BANG!

Look Back at *At Home*

CHECK YOUR UNDERSTANDING

1. What does each person in the family do for Grandmother?

2. How can you tell that Grandmother feels glad?

3. What are some special things that you do for your family?

WORD WORK: Long Vowels

Find all the words with a long vowel and silent e.

Make a list. Compare your list to your partner's list. Read the two lists aloud. Did you find the same words?

hope	bake
time	tune

My grandmother is here from Japan. Our family is glad to see her. We hope she likes our home.

Soon it is time to eat. We use our best dishes for the food. We take out the best glasses. Then we sit down and eat together. Grandmother smiles and smiles.

I like this food! The cake is good, too!

3

It smells good!

We want to make Grandmother glad that she came to see us. So we think of special things to do for her. In Japan, Grandmother does not bake cakes. So I make her one.

My mother makes crab rolls for Grandmother.

We really like these. I hope she will, too.

My brother wants to do something, too. So he writes some notes for a new tune.

Will Grandmother like this song?

My father puts on his fine silk robe.

Mother will like this.

Long Vowels: ai, ay; ee, ea; oa, ow and Compound Words

On the River

It's the end of the day.

Well, we don't have any fish.

No, but we had a neat day, and it didn't rain!

Look Back at On the River

CHECK YOUR UNDERSTANDING

1. Why does Shane's granddad take him to the river?

2. What kinds of animals do Shane and his granddad see?

3. Do you think Shane has a good time on the river? Tell why or why not.

WORD WORK: Long e

Find all the words in the story with the long e sound. Circle them. Then write each word on an index card. Put all the words spelled with ee in one group. Put all the words spelled with ea in another group. Read the cards aloud to a partner.

weekend

eat

Is that rain?

I don't think so.

In late June, Shane always spends a weekend with his granddad. This year Granddad takes him to Greenstone River. It's a good place to fish. You can also see a lot of wildlife there.

It's almost sunset. Still no fish. Shane asks if fish like this spot.

Fish like deep water. Once I caught a trout this big here.

Granddad knows the best places to find fish.

I can show you where the rainbow trout swim.

Did you get a bite?

Not yet.

They wait for the fish to bite. While they wait, Shane sees something.

Look!

That's a bald eagle! It hunts for small animals that live by the water. It eats fish, too.

4

Shane hears something in the cattail plants.

Look at the toad!

That's a tree frog. Frogs can be hard to spot. They sleep in the daytime.

5

Verb Ending -ed

About Duke

Hi, Duke! How are you? How is your new home?

Chen, do I need to tell you again? Your dog is just fine!

WOOF!

Look Back at *About Duke*

CHECK YOUR UNDERSTANDING

1. Who is Duke?

2. Why does Chen miss him?

3. How do you think Chen felt after he talked to Duke? What will Chen do next?

WORD WORK: Verb Ending -ed

Circle all the verbs that end with -ed. Underline the root words. Then read each word to a partner. How many different sounds for -ed does your partner hear?

Verbs That End with -ed

waited   liked
jogged   hunted

Before I came here, Duke and I were always together. He waited for me after school. He was there to greet me when I stepped off the bus.

We love books. Let's find some books to read together.

Duke even liked to sit with me and look at books.

LIBRARY

LIBRARY

Fold

Verb Ending -*ing*

Celebrate the Past

Children are singing as we leave the fair. I look back, wondering if we really went into the past.

It's fun to celebrate the past this way!

Look Back at *Celebrate the Past*

CHECK YOUR UNDERSTANDING

Make a concept map to tell about the Old English Fair.

Old English Fair

Food

Things to Do

dress up in costumes

WORD WORK: Verb Ending -*ing*

Circle the verbs in the story that end in -*ing*. Write the words in a chart.

Add -*ing*	Drop silent e and add -*ing*	Double the consonant and add -*ing*
dressing	taking	scrubbing

My friends are taking me to a fair. It is like a trip back in time.

This seems like a city in old England.

A play is beginning, and the actors are speaking to me! They ask me to come on the stage and be the queen!

People are dressing in costumes. We want to dress up, too. Sam has a velvet cap. Todd is pinning a ribbon on another hat.

We are eating very odd food today. Todd is tasting something called "toad in the hole." I am feasting on "beef on a stick."

They are playing tunes just like people played 400 years ago! A young man is twirling sticks.

Some women are scrubbing clothes in a stream. They are joking and slapping the cloth on rocks.

I like the way they talk.

I do, too. They speak the way people spoke long ago.

RESCUE at the BEACH

Thanks! You tried to warn me. You are a great lifeguard!

Look Back at *Rescue at the Beach*

CHECK YOUR UNDERSTANDING

1. Why does Ann get into trouble?

2. How does Deb rescue Ann?

3. What do you think Ann will do the next time she tries surfing?

WORD WORK: Long Vowels

Circle all the words in the story with the long *i* sound. Underline all the words in the story with the long *u* sound.

Write the words in the chart. Write each word one time.

ie	igh	ui	ue
skies	bright	suit	blue

The skies are blue and the water feels great.
Ann and Kim plan to have a good day at the
beach. They meet Deb on the sand.

Hi, Deb. I like
your bright
red suit.

Thanks, Ann! It's
my lifeguard suit.

This time, Ann listens. She does
what Deb tells her.
Deb meets Ann and helps her to
the shore.

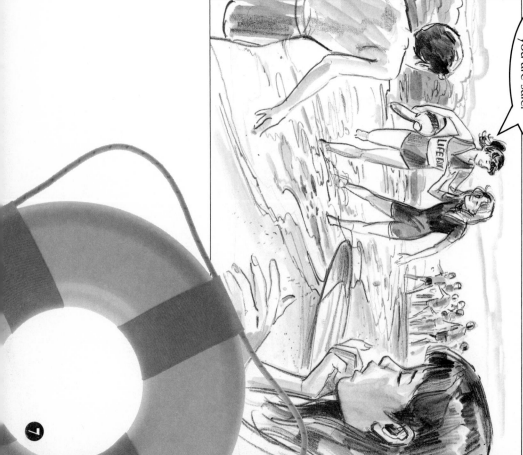

You gave me a
fright! I'm glad
you are safe.

2

7

Ann is surprised that Deb is a lifeguard. Kim isn't.

I hope she never needs to rescue me.

It's true that Deb is small, but she is a really strong swimmer.

Ann tries to fight the wave. Another high wave is coming. Deb yells to Ann. She tells Ann **what to do.**

Don't fight the wave! Let the next wave bring you in!

DANGER
KEEP AWAY
FROM ROCKS

4

Ann is in a rush to get in the water and start surfing. She is between the waves and the rocks. She doesn't see the sign about the rocks. Deb tells her to watch out.

Ann doesn't listen to Deb. Then a big wave takes her close to the rocks. She needs help! Deb runs as fast as she can.

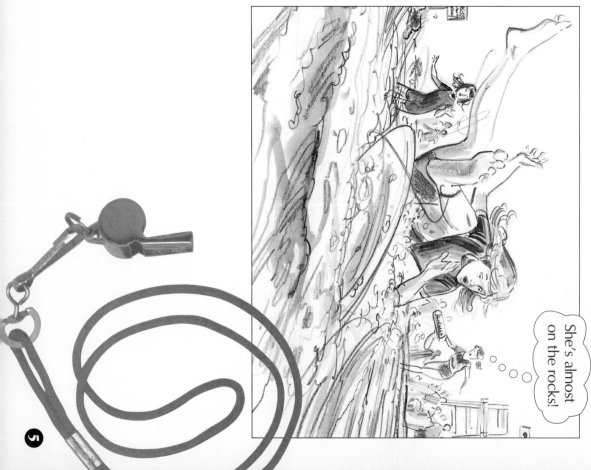

5

Community Bulletin Board

Teens Reach Out and Recycle

We need things for our yard sale NOW! Chairs, tools, games, skirts, shirts, French horns! Don't throw them away. We can use them! Call 555-9146.

Look Back at Community Bulletin Board

CHECK YOUR UNDERSTANDING

1. Which group helps animals?

2. Which happens first, the concert or the car wash?

3. Which way of helping sounds good to you? Tell why.

WORD WORK: R-Controlled Vowels

Work in a group of three. Choose one of these words: *star, year, chair.* Work with your partners to think of words that rhyme with your word. Write the words on index cards.

star

year

chair

All around the world, teens use their time and skills to help others. Teens in this country are no different. American teens use their skills to make the world a better place. Look around your city for a community bulletin board like the one on these pages. Find your own way to make a difference!

Are you a star at math?

Help at The Homework Place.

Get $6.00 an hour.

861 First Street

Ask for Bert.

CONCERT IN THE BARN
MAY 1

Bring your earplugs!

The Hard Rock Boys are doing a concert to raise money for three children hurt in a fire this year. The star of the show will be **Mark Jones.** This is your last chance to hear him play before he moves to New York.

Car Wash
$5.00
We get the dirt off!

**Help our school band take
a trip to Bear Mountain.**

Bring your car to Park School,
10 Park Drive, on March 30.

(Go north on Fern Lane. Turn right on Park Drive. Park at the curb.)

Be an Artist for the Day

Make Art
in the Park

March 31

You can **paint**. You can **weave** or
make a **clay pot**. Funds will be used to
add a room to Deerfield Senior Center.

The Perfect Moose

The perfect moose may live for as long as 12 years.

Look Back at *The Perfect Moose*

CHECK YOUR UNDERSTANDING

1. Where do moose live?

2. What happens to the male moose in the winter and spring?

3. Look back at the article. Pick one interesting fact you learned. Share it with a partner.

WORD WORK:
R-Controlled Syllables

Work with a partner. Find words with these syllables.

per   ber   mer
for   ter   der

Both of you write each word on an index card. Take turns reading the words aloud. Hold up the word your partner reads.

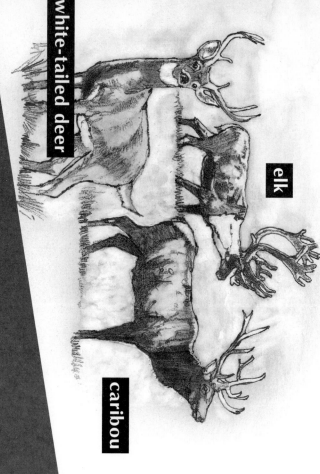

white-tailed deer

elk

caribou

The moose is a member of the deer family. The white-tailed deer, the elk, and the caribou are part of this same family. Members of the deer family live in many parts of the world.

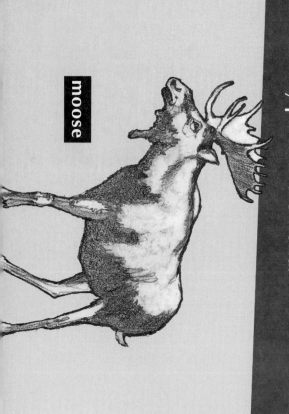

moose

2

A grown moose does not fear attack because it is so big. A wolf pack or a bear may attack a calf or a moose that is sick, but not one that is grown and strong.

wolf

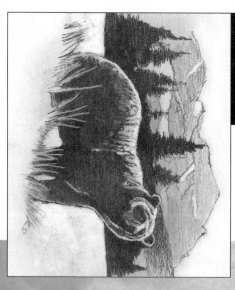

brown bear

7

Moose live in northern mountains and forests. A mother is called a cow. A baby is called a calf. Calves are born in the spring and stay with the mother for a year. Then the mother chases them away, and they must survive on their own.

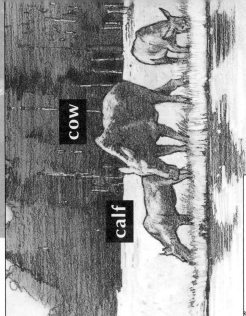

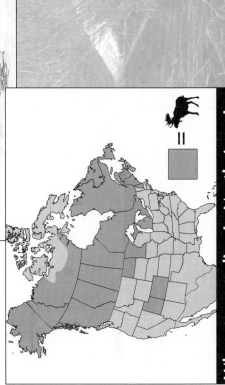

Where moose live in North America

3

Moose like water and are expert swimmers. They wade in ponds and lakes to eat the plants that grow under the water. They also eat twigs and shrubs on land. Moose will not hunt animals, but some animals hunt them.

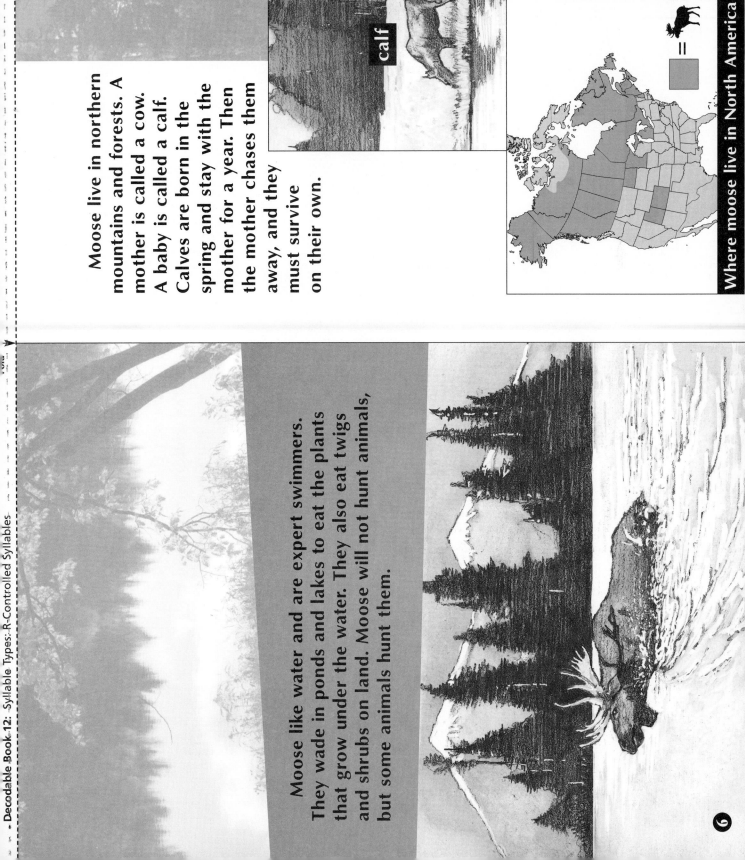

6

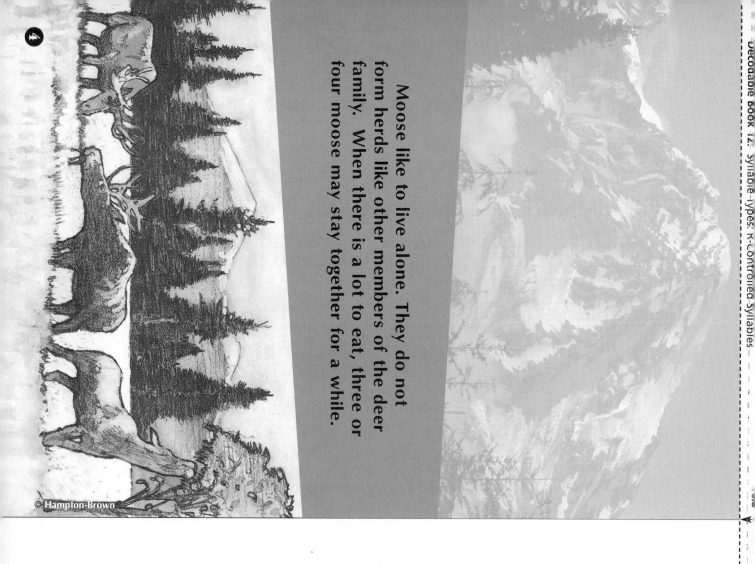

© Hampton-Brown

Moose like to live alone. They do not form herds like other members of the deer family. When there is a lot to eat, three or four moose may stay together for a while.

The male, or bull, has big antlers. He uses the antlers to fight other bulls during mating time. Bulls shed the antlers in the winter and grow new antlers in the spring.

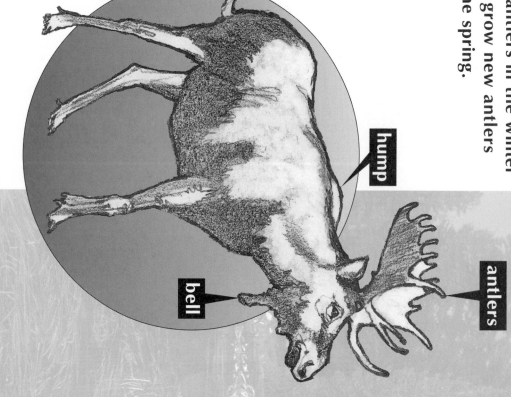

hump

bell

antlers

Kathy's Diary

© Hampton-Brown

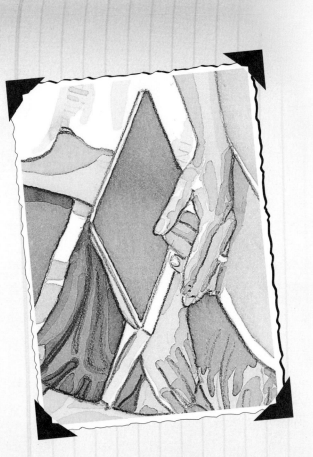

Look Back at Kathy's Diary

CHECK YOUR UNDERSTANDING

1. How does Kathy feel in the first diary entry? How does she feel in her last entry?

2. What did people do on the day the war ended?

3. Do you think Kathy's diary is interesting? Tell why or why not.

WORD WORK: Words with y

Make a list of all the words in the story that end in y. Write each word in a chart one time.

y sounds like the long i in	y sounds like the long e in
sky	study

Back in 1945, Kathy Grady started a diary. She wrote about her life during that time.

Each page Kathy wrote is called an entry. Here are some entries from Kathy's diary.

In 1960, Kathy is all grown up. She has two children of her own. She reads her diary to them. Her kids like to hear about life in the 1940s. It seems like a long time ago, but the words in Kathy's diary bring the past to life.

Daddy went to Italy three years ago. He is in the Army Air Force. He flies a big plane called a B-42.

This picture shows my dad with some of his buddies. Dad is the second man on the right. We miss him so much!

My dad is home!

One of his Army buddies is with him. We feel so lucky to have him back! Mom is happier than ever. She is going to make french fries and hamburgers. They are Dad's favorite foods.

Some nights we sit and study
the sky. We are watching for our
boys to fly home. Many of them
have been away for four years!

People say the war may
end soon! We all wait for
that happy day.

The war is over! People are
yelling and waving flags. You can
hear their cries of joy. We all
act silly. Mom is playing music
and dancing.

I rushed out to get a
newspaper. Dad can read it
when he gets home.

Diphthongs and Variant Vowels

A Pinch of Salt

The neighbors clapped with joy. At last, they all sat down to eat. They chatted and joked and ate lots of stew, just as they always did.

Look Back at *A Pinch of Salt*

CHECK YOUR UNDERSTANDING

1. How does the woman make the stew?

2. What do the neighbors add to the stew?

3. The story says the woman was wise. Do you agree? Why or why not?

WORD WORK: Diphthongs and Variant Vowels

Say the name of each picture.

Find words in the story with the same vowel sound. Write them on cards. Compare the cards. How many ways is the vowel sound spelled?

Once there was a wise woman named Mrs. Paul. She lived in a small house at the end of town. She was not rich, but all her neighbors loved her. One morning the woman saw that her cupboard was empty. She found only a few peas to eat. She was too proud to beg, but she was too smart to stay hungry.

She put the peas into the pot. She filled the pot with water. Then she put the pot over the fire, just as she always did.

It was time for the woman to add one last thing, just as she always did. She added a pinch of salt. She stirred the pot, then tasted the stew again.

Perfect!

When the pot began
to simmer and steam, she
called to her neighbors.

Join me for a
pot of stew!

Thank you!

We will
join you!

All the neighbors heard her call.
They nodded and smiled, just as they
always did.

The woman tasted
the stew. She frowned.

This stew
tastes awful!

The neighbors smiled and
waited, just as they always did.

4

Soon, a crowd of neighbors entered her house. They each added food to the pot. They added carrots, meat, onions, and more peas. They filled the pot to the brim, just as they always did.

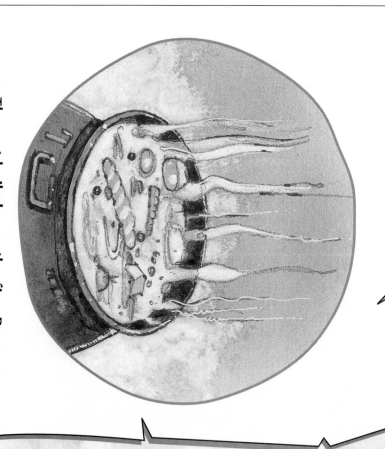

The pot boiled over the fire. By noon, the smell of rich stew filled the small house. It made the neighbors hungry.

A Good Game

Mel   Gene   Rick

He skates, and he falls. He falls, and he skates. He falls twice in a row, but he's such a good sport. Gene's friends knew he would have fun at hockey!

Can't I just hit the puck from here?

Sure!

Look Back at A Good Game

CHECK YOUR UNDERSTANDING

1. Why do Mel and Rick take Gene to the ice rink?

2. How does Gene show he is a good sport?

3. Do you think Mel and Rick are good friends to Gene? Tell why or why not.

WORD WORK: Words with c or g

Work with a partner. Circle all the words in the story that have the letter g. Have your partner circle all the words in the story with the letter c. Write your words on index cards. See how many words your partner can read in 7 seconds. Then it's your turn to try.

good

Gene's friends take him to the ice rink to play hockey. There are kids on the ice already. They are playing a game. This is Gene's first time on skates.

I don't know about this!

Come on. You'll do fine!

We're your friends. We'll help you.

Gene looks at the other kids. They are moving so fast! At last, Gene gets on the ice. He puts one foot in front of the other. He's on his feet, and he's skating!

Gene sits at the edge of the ice. While he puts on his skates, he watches the players on the ice. Some of them are huge!

Mel wants to be sure Gene is safe.

The boys are ready to play. Mel shows Gene the puck. Rick gives him the wooden stick.
Gene does not think he will be good at hockey.

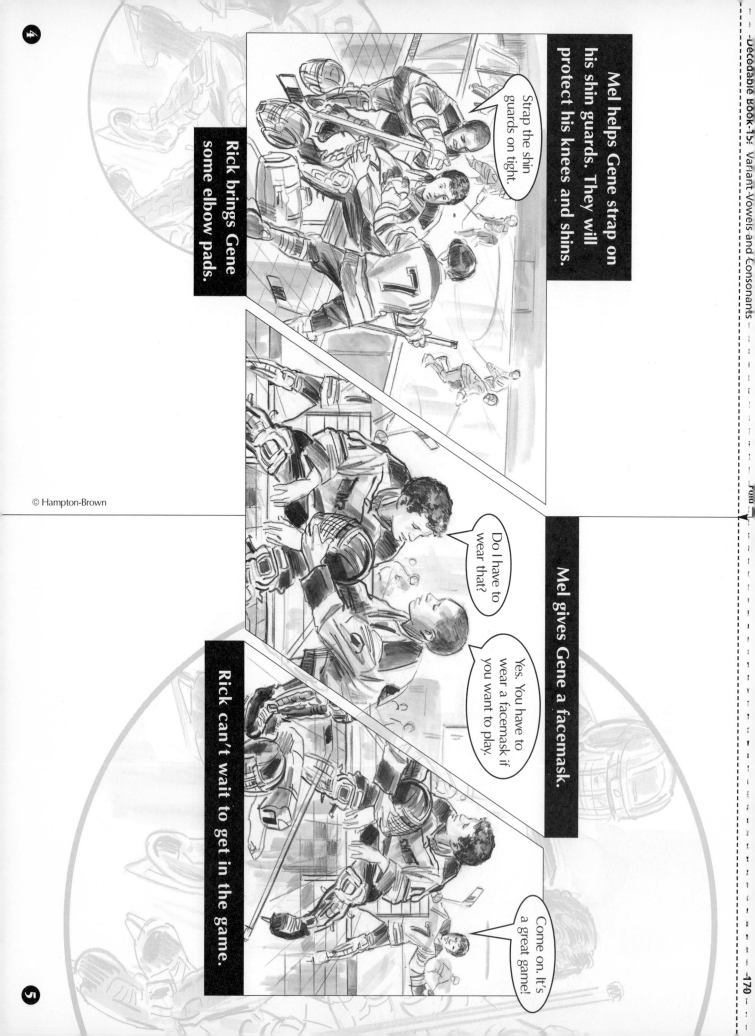

Mel helps Gene strap on his shin guards. They will protect his knees and shins.

Strap the shin guards on tight.

Rick brings Gene some elbow pads.

Mel gives Gene a facemask.

Do I have to wear that?

Yes. You have to wear a facemask if you want to play.

Rick can't wait to get in the game.

Come on. It's a great game!

POSTCARDS from DEVEN

Arizona
New Mexico

Southwestern States

U.S.OFFIC
U.S. POST

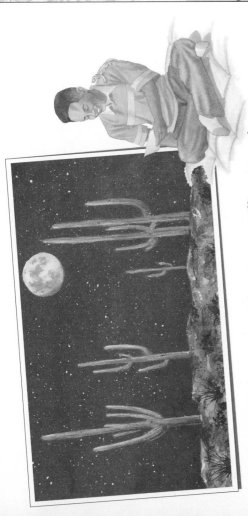

Last night we camped under a million stars!
A coyote howled at the moon. Dad told funny stories
about cowboys in the desert. I think we laughed for
hours. I want to come back here soon.

See you next week. I have a lot of pictures to
show you.

Look Back at *Postcards from Deven*

CHECK YOUR UNDERSTANDING

1. Name three of the places Deven went. Tell what he saw at each place.

2. Tell about Deven's night in the desert.

3. What type of things did Deven do on his vacation?

WORD WORK: Multisyllabic Words

canyon	explore	hundreds
awake	around	cabin
music	even	until

Copy each word on one side of a card. On the back write its syllables. Show the card to a partner. Have your partner blend the syllables and tell you the word.

Hey, Brent! I am at Four Corners. This is the place where four states share a border. It is the only place in the U.S. like this. I stood on all four states at one time! Dad took a great picture of me.

Four Corners

Utah

Arizona

Colorado

New Mexico

I am reading a good book about the Anasazi. I could not put it down last night. I was awake until midnight!

Today, we just relaxed in our cabin. I was so tired. Dad got us big burritos for lunch.

There's a country-western music show later. I am going to dance and dance!

Cabin near Flagstaff, Arizona

EXPLORE AMAZING UTAH!

Today, we went hiking in the mountains near Four Corners. It was hot in the valley below. We walked for three hours to get to the top. It's so high up there! You can see for miles! It was much cooler, too. We even had to wear our jackets.

3

White Water Rafting in Arizona

This is the most amazing place on Earth! We went rafting on the river. The red and brown canyon walls around us are taller than my house. The river took us over fast rapids. The water was very cold. It felt great in the hot sun.

6

Wow! This place is great. There are thousands of big red rocks here. Some look like skyscrapers and bridges, too. You need to see them sometime. I didn't want to leave.

Arches National Monument, Utah

Today, we got to explore some cliff dwellings. The Anasazi people built them hundreds of years ago. There are many rooms in the cliffs. In fact, the rooms form a village. There are ladders that go into some of the rooms. Some rooms have round towers.

Mesa Verde, Colorado

Fold

The Orchard

Late at night, I go outside and think about my great-grandfather. I'm so happy to share the gift he left my family so long ago.

Look Back at *The Orchard*

CHECK YOUR UNDERSTANDING

1. What gift did the great-grandfather give to his family?

2. Tell the different ways the family enjoys this gift.

3. Think of a gift a family member gave you. How is it like Great-grandfather's gift? How is it different?

WORD WORK: Prefixes and Suffixes

Find the words in the story that mean:

not ripe
use again
without end
not like
full of harm
in a careful way

Write the words and read them to a partner.

My family has a beautiful peach orchard. My great-grandfather planted the trees as a special gift to his family. Every summer, we all gather to pick the plump fruit from the trees. We are very thankful for the trees.

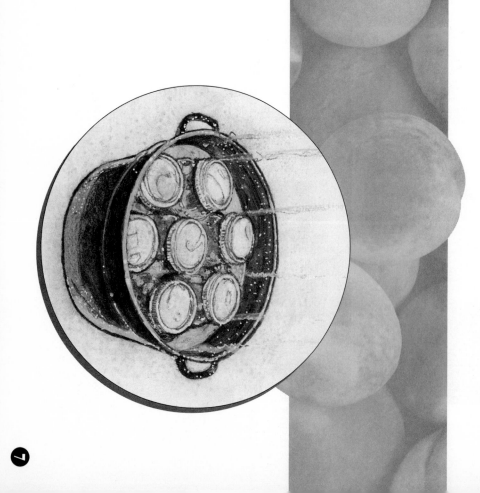

We boil the filled jars. This kills any harmful bacteria in the fruit. After the jars cool, we label each one.

Our canned fruit is unlike anything you buy in a store. Sometimes when we give a jar away, the people bring back the empty jar and ask for a refill!

We wait all year for the peaches to grow. In the late winter, small pink buds appear on the trees. The flowers blossom. Then the petals fall off and float silently to the ground. In the spring, the fuzzy peaches start to form. We set up a big picnic table near the branches full of hard, unripe fruit. We all eat together under the shade of the trees.

Only a few more weeks until the peaches are ripe!

We sit and listen. The leaves flutter softly in the wind. It is like Great-grandfather's voice whispering that we will soon enjoy his gift.

Dad gently washes each peach. I peel the skin and remove the pits. Mom carefully packs the fruit into the jars and covers it with cupfuls of warm, sticky syrup. Then we screw on each lid tightly.

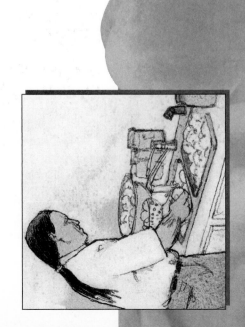

When summer is finally here, there is endless work outdoors. All of the family and countless friends arrive. Everyone is so helpful. We carry crates and pick the healthy fruit.

We have a lot of fresh peaches, so we put some in jars to enjoy in the winter.

When it's time to can the fruit, there is endless work indoors. We unpack boxes of glass jars that we reuse from year to year. We still have a few jars from when Great-grandmother canned peaches years ago!

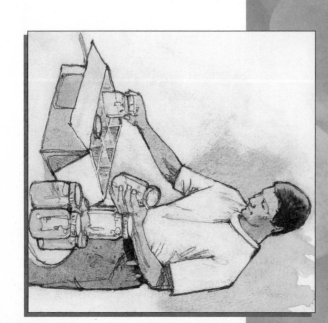

Meteor Shower

The Geminids will come again next year, too. Look for them. If the sky is clear, you will be amazed, too!

Look Back at Meteor Shower

CHECK YOUR UNDERSTANDING

1. What is a meteor?

2. Why does the boy take his friends to the top of a hill on December 13?

3. Why will they always remember this night?

WORD WORK: Multisyllabic Words

Find 5 words with two syllables. Write each word on a strip of paper. Cut each word into syllables. Scramble the strips of paper. Then ask a partner to match the syllables and read the word aloud.

mid	dle
sea	son

It's the middle of the night on December 13. It is winter, the darkest season of the year. My friends wonder what I am going to show them. They grumble as we trudge up the steep hill.

What a fantastic way to celebrate the darkest season of the year! My friends and I will always remember this night.

3

I smile and lead them up the hill. I did not tell them what is going to happen. I want them to be surprised. I know they will enjoy the show. I check my watch. It's eleven p.m. The night sky will soon be filled with hundreds of shooting stars, or meteors, whizzing past the earth. I can hardly wait.

Look! Look!

6

Suddenly hundreds of meteors begin to shoot across the sky. It's like a fireworks display! My friends do not grumble anymore. They are really glad they came. We huddle beneath blankets and watch the amazing show.

Meteors are bits of space dirt. They hurtle through space at great speeds. Some pass very close to Earth. They burn up in the layer of gas that surrounds the planet. Meteors look like bright balls of fire as they burn. Most burn out and then fall to the earth as dust.

Sometimes a meteor does not burn up and crashes into Earth with a great bang! That does not happen very often.

The meteor shower begins right on time. My friends are excited to see the first shooting star. I do not tell them that there will be more— many more.

Look! A shooting star!

Yes! There's another one! Where do they come from?

These meteors are called Geminids because they appear to come from a group of stars called Gemini. I look in the sky for that group of stars. I tell my friends that Gemini means "The Twins" in Latin. I point to The Twins in the night sky.

Acknowledgments

Photographs

pp39, 40: courtesy of Elaine Soares

p93: Zoran Milich

Book Divider Tabs: 1-3, Liz Garza Williams

Artville: pp2, 4, 6-10, pp12-13, 15-16, 18-19, 21-22, 24-26, 29, 33, 39-40, 44, 48, 51-52, 56, 59, 63, 75, 78, 79, 94, 106, 140

Bruce Coleman Inc.: p66

Corbis: p3 ©Corbis, p16 ©Laura Dewight, p19 ©Elaine Soares, ©Laura Dewight, p20 ©William Sallaz, p22 ©Laura Dewight, ©William Sallaz, p24 ©Laura Dewight, p25 ©Elaine Soares, ©Laura Dewight, ©William Sallaz, p30 ©Rojer Kessmeyer, p32 ©Elaine Soares, ©Rojer Kessmeyer, p33 ©Elaine Soares, ©Rojer Kessmeyer, p36 ©Dennis di Cicco, p40 ©Michael Yamashita, ©William Sallaz, p47 ©Anthony Nex, p51 ©Leonard de Selva / Corbis, ©Lewis Philppa, p56 ©Leonard de Selva / Corbis, p60 ©Michael Dunn, p63 ©Forest Johnson, ©Bruce Hands, ©Ariel Skelley, p65 ©Pat O'Hara / Corbis, p78 ©Lee Snider, p85 ©M.Dillon / Corbis, p96 ©David Muench / Corbis, p98 ©Bettmann / Corbis, p102 ©Corbis, p107 ©Layne Kennedy, p140 ©The Purcell Team

Corbis Stock Market: p18 ©Thom Lang, p47 ©Phillip Walker, p47 ©Phillip Warlick, p48 ©David Keaton, p72 ©Ariel Skelley, p82 ©John P. Endress, ©David Sailors, p102 ©Lester Lefkowitz, p103 ©David Pollack, p107 ©Corbis

Corel: p63

Digital Stock: pp51, 140

Digital Studios: pp4, 21, 22, 26

EyeWire: pp3, 4, 7 ©1998-2001 EyeWire, Inc., p10 ©Ryan McVay, p13 ©Ryan McVay, pp15, 19 ©Ryan McVay, pp48, 55, 85

Food Pix: p82 ©Brian Hagiwara

FPG International: p59 ©Estephan Simpson, p63 ©Laurence B. Aluppi, p64 ©FPG International, p65 ©FPG International, p78 ©Larry West, p85 ©Peter Gridley, p97 ©Paul & Lindamarie Ambruse, p101 ©Ken Ross, ©Barbara Peacock

Getty Images: p82 ©1999-2000 Getty Images, Inc., p85 ©David Paul Productions, p140 ©Paul & Lindamarie Ambrose, p141 ©Tony Anderson, ©Mike McQueen, ©PhotoDisc

Grant Heilman Photography: p63 ©Arthur C. Smith III, p101 ©Grant Heilman Photography

Image Bank: p3 ©Harald Sund, p44 ©Alfred Gescheidt, p48 ©Bob Elsdale, p97 ©Rita Maas, p141 ©Rita Maas

Image Club: p47 ©Image Club, p93 ©Image Club

John Paul Endress: pp9-10, 12-13, 15-16, 18-19, 22, 25, 28, 30-34, 36, 43-44, 47-48, 56, 59-60, 65, 75, 78, 82, 85, 93, 97, 101, 103, 106-107, 140-141

Liz Garza Williams: pp1, 3, 5-10, 12-13, 15-19, 21-25, 28, 30-34, 36, 40-41, 43-45, 47, 55, 57, 60-61, 63, 93, 97, 103, 140

New Century Graphics: pp30, 33, 43-44

Object Gear: pp3-4, 9, 24-25, 30, 32-33, 47, 60, 103

PhotoDisc: p3 ©Ryan McVay, ©Steve Cole, ©Paul Bread, p4 ©Steve Cole, ©Paul Bread, pp6-9, ©Janis Christie, p10, p12-13 ©Paul Bread, p15 ©Spike, p16, ©C Squared Studios, p19 p24 ©C Squared Studios, ©Ryan McVay, p25 ©C Squared Studios, p29-30, P32 ©Ryan McVay, p33 ©C Squared Studios, ©Paul Bread, p39-40, p43-44 ©Javier Pierini, p48, p51-52 ©Steve Mason, p55-56, p59-60, p63-64 ©Nancy R. Cohen, p65, p72, p78 ©Jess Alford, p79 ©Ryan McVay, ©Jules Frazier, p82 ©Ryan McVay, p93 ©Lawrence Lawry, p94, p97, p98, p101-103, p106-107, p140 ©Barbara Penovar, ©C Squared Studios, p141 ©C Squared Studios, ©Ryan McVay

PhotoEdit: p15 ©Felisha Martinez, ©Michael Newman, p24 ©David Young-Wolff, p25 ©David Young-Wolff, p47 ©Myrleen Ferguson Cate / PhotoEdit, ©David Young-Wolff, ©Billy E. Barnes, ©Michael Newman, p48 ©Robert Bremnel, p49 ©Rudi Von Briel, p56 ©Michael Newman, p63 ©Felisha Martinez, p64 ©David Young-Wolff, p97 ©PhotoEdit, p102, ©Myrleen Ferguson Cate, ©Bonnie Kamin, p107 ©David Young-Wolff, ©Myrleen Ferguson Cate, ©Bill Bachmann, p140 ©Peter Byron, ©Tony Freeman, p141 ©David Young-Wolff

Photo Researchers Inc.: p63 ©Joe Monroe, ©Peter Arnold, p64 ©Okapia Frankfurt, p65 ©Peter Arnold, p75 ©Photo Researchers, p98 ©David Ducros, p141 ©John Foster

PictureQuest: p79 ©Fransisco Erize / Bruce Coleman, Inc., p94 ©Carol Christenson, p97 ©PhotoSphere Images, p98 ©Digital Vision

Sports Chrome: p93

Stockbyte: p9-10, p12-13, p15-16, p18-19, p33, p141

Stock Food: p48 ©Eising Food Photography

Stone: p22 ©Charles Krebs, p25 ©Charles Krebs, p40 ©Stone / Michael Lang, ©Stone / James Balog, p47 ©Louis Grandadam, p48 ©Peter Cortez, p52 ©Stone / James Balog, p65 ©Waren Bolster, p79 ©Paul Dance, p93 ©Robert Daly, p97 ©Camille Tokerud, p98 ©Robert Daly, p106 ©Stone, p141 ©Mike McQueen

Superstock: p9 p59-60, p63-64, p140

Woodfin Camp & Associates: p15 ©Ken Heyman, p30 ©Ken Heyman, p32 ©Ken Heyman

Illustrations

Marcia J. Bateman Walker: pp151-154, **Norm Bendell:** p53, p70, **Chi Chung:** p21, **Alex von Dallwitz:** p63, **Liisa Chauncey Guida:** p6-7, **Judith DuFour Love:** p30, p74, p86, **Maurie Manning:** p68-69, **Den Schofield:** pp143-146, pp179-182, **Michael Slack:** p2, p5, p7, p11, p21, **Dick Smolinski:** pp111-114, pp115-118, pp119-122, pp123-126, pp127-130, pp131-133, pp139-142, **Frank Sofo:** pp147-150, pp167-170, **Ken Stetz:** pp159-162, **Stephen Wells:** pp171-174, **Lee Woolry:** pp135-140, pp155-158, pp163-166, pp175-178

THE HIGH POINT DEVELOPMENT TEAM

Hampton-Brown extends special thanks to the following individuals and companies who contributed so much to the creation of this book.

Design and Production:

Marcia J. Bateman Walker, Matthew K. Brown, Aaron D. Busch, Alex von Dallwitz, Terry Harmon, Davis I Hernandez, Connie McPhedran, Deborah Miller, Russell Nemec, Roger Rybkowski, Debbie Saxton, Curtis Spitler, Margaret E. Tisdale, Donna L. Turner, JR Walker

Editorial:

Shirleyann Costigan, Kellie Crain, Phyllis Edwards, Suzanne Gardner, Fredrick Ignacio, Dawn Liseth, Sheron Long, Jacalyn Mahler, Michele McFadden, Debbi Neel, Elizabeth Sengel, Sharon Ursino, Lynn Yokoe